Soccer Alive
The Game is the Best Teacher

P66 SHOOTING
P63 COMMUNICATIONS
P188 SHOOTING
P184 -185 FINISHING

Detlev Brueggemann

SOCCER ALIVE

THE GAME IS THE BEST TEACHER

Game-related Soccer Training

"Those who can play 3 on 3 successfully can play soccer!"
César Luis Menotti

British Library Cataloguing in Publication Data
A catalogue record for this book is available from the British Library

Detlev Brueggemann
Soccer Alive - The Game is the Best Teacher
Maidenhead: Meyer & Meyer Sport (UK) Ltd., 2008
ISBN 978-1-84126-235-2

© 2008 by Meyer & Meyer Sport (UK) Ltd.
Aachen, Adelalde, Auckland, Budapest, Cape Town, Graz, Indianapolis,
Maidenhead, New York, Olten (CH), Singapore, Toronto
Member of the World
Sport Publishers' Association (WSPA)
www.w-s-p-a.org

Printed and bound by: B.O.S.S Druck und Medien GmbH, Germany
ISBN 978-1-84126-235-2
E-Mail: verlag@m-m-sports.com
www.m-m-sports.com

CONTENT

Credits:
Cover Photo: dpa Picture Alliance
Back Cover Photo: getty images
Cover Design: Jens Vogelsang
Photos & Freeze Frames: Detlev Brueggemann
Illustrations: Peter Schreiner, easy sports Software
Editing by: Frank Tschan

THE GAME IS THE BEST TEACHER

Detlev Brueggemann

**For the Good of Soccer
(The author)**

"The children are just playing" is a complaint some people make when observing boys and girls practicing soccer within small-sided games (i.e. 4 vs. 4) in a training session. "Training should be drills, technical and physical drills, in order to play the game successfully."

"We spend so much money on our children's training sessions that we expect them to get efficient training instead of just playing." Some parents, like these, worry about the lack of drills. Others criticize teachers and coaches for practicing with mostly games. "How are children going to learn to play soccer?"

Do you really believe the game of soccer can be learned most efficiently by drills, highly-organized repetitions of special movements, like track and field athletes or gymnasts have to do in practice?

Former FIFA soccer coach Dettmar Cramer, whose experience includes having worked within more than 90 different countries all over the world and having coached both professional and national teams, once said: "Soccer can be learned only by playing soccer!"

Where do we find the roots of the outstanding performances of so many top soccer players? How did Zinedine Zidane of France, Ronaldinho of Brazil, Drogba of the Ivory Coast, Riquelme of Argentina, Beckham of England and so many others begin to learn the game of soccer?

Why do so many talented young soccer players who live in countries without advanced soccer schools, structured training sessions and experienced coaches still achieve top level as international professionals?

This first volume of the set of books **"SOCCER ALIVE" - The Game Is the Best Teacher** presents an answer. This answer is the new didactical approach for training. "The game is the best teacher." Based on this philosophy, the essential demands of soccer are addressed. The first and most crucial demand requires players to practice **what is needed and how it is needed in the game**.

> PLAYERS AND GOALKEEPERS SHOULD PRACTICE
>
> WHAT IS NEEDED IN THE GAME AND
>
> HOW IT IS NEEDED IN THE GAME

Instructors, coaches and experts all over the world agree that speed determines the quality of a player and a game to a very high degree. Speed in this sense does not only mean the pace a player can achieve. Speed includes reaction and the power to start, to turn or to stop. Generally speaking, the fastest player in the game will be the one who is able to decide at once when and how to act. The capability of reading the game relates to the mental ability of making quick decisions. This includes knowing where to run, how to play the ball and to whom and, in particular, when to support and to act. For many years, training did not really pay attention to the decision-making factor required in such a quick game. However, the use of all technical and tactical abilities in the game is always connected to the ability to make decisions.

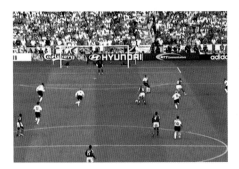

The ball carrier has to decide immediately because each second lost gives time for the defenders to slow down the attack.

The ball carrier (10) has to decide:

- to dribble on his own in order to finish
- to pass into the run of his supporting teammate to the right
- to shoot immediately any defender can block a shot or challenge him.

Today the most likely reason can be pointed out, why players are not as successful in the game, although they have practiced a movement many times with an obvious progression. In contrast to many typical training exercises, the performance of each technical, tactical, or even physical movement must be strictly linked to the particular game situation and the players' decisions in order to successfully execute an action in the match. This means that the abilities needed in soccer should be practiced within an environment which is clearly related to real-game situations. It is not the exercises themselves which have to be practiced, but rather the successful application of the behaviors found within those game-related exercises.

Volume I of the set **"SOCCER ALIVE" - The Game Is the Best Teacher** is the first ever soccer book to truly teach the methods based on this philosophy. It presents the new didactical approach of using game situations to improve particular movements and behaviors which are most frequently used during the game. This volume explains how to deal with game situations as a model for appropriate exercises and how to coach players practicing complex tasks. The book is geared towards the training of children and players at lower levels.

> COACHING SHOULD ALWAYS BE
> FACT-RELATED

Volume II of this set will describe how to implement this new approach for advanced training. Dedicated to the level of highly experienced and professional players, topics like training in groups, systems in attack and defense, set plays and physical training are selected in order to build on the basics of Volume 1.

There is a need for coaching soccer based on facts. Don't just tell the player what you want him to do, show him and allow him to experience it. The focus must be on the game situation, incorporating teammates' and opponents' expected behaviors.

FOREWORD

The concept of "bridging the gap" between training and the game itself is a fundamental challenge for soccer coaches at all levels. All too often we hear about skills which players execute near to perfection in training, but don't seem to be able to replicate during the match itself on a consistent enough basis. The fundamental question one consequently raises then focuses on the extent to which the training environment replicates the game environment. Many coaches today find themselves working in environments characterized by either highly organized, pre-determined, rote drills or simply rolling the ball out and letting the children play. However, as we know the game is actually neither of these, but rather a player-centered sport which does indeed require a certain level of influence from external sources, i.e. the coach.

Somewhere in the space between these two extremes lies the ultimate approach to coaching soccer. This "gap" as I call it, needs to be properly evaluated and "bridged" in order for individual players and teams to transition from training to the game and back again most effectively.

Soccer Alive is one of the first books of its kind dedicated to literally using the game as the driving force behind the training session. In his latest publication, FIFA and DFB Master Coach Detlev Brueggemann clearly and effectively demonstrates how to extract specific moments of a game to create goal-oriented, developmentally appropriate and progressive training sessions. His attention to the intricacies of both playing and coaching soccer cannot be underestimated. Using the priorities of training based on players needs (as opposed to coaches' strengths), selecting activities which focus on multiple abilities simultaneously and the concept of transition as one of major importance, Coach Brueggemann successfully provides the coach unlimited tools for teaching the technical and tactical components of the soccer in a purely game-related environment.

Soccer Alive is a user-friendly resource which engages the reader via full-color photos of top level matches in which specific scenarios are depicted. From there, a simple diagram reproduces the image from the picture, after which the desired exercise is further diagrammed and explained. Perhaps most important, however, are the many modifications and restrictions recommended to match the activity to the level of the player.

The globalization of soccer in modern society has led to enormous opportunity for coaches to gain access to the game around the world. Coach Detlev Brueggemann, one of the world's most traveled coaches, has taken a culmination of his many experiences coaching players and coaches on nearly every continent and presented them here for all of us to benefit from.

Frank Tschan
Director of Coaching Education: ODP Europe
NSCAA Associate Staff Member
Director of Sports: International School of Düsseldorf, Germany

FOREWORD

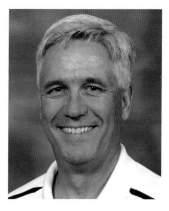

In some parts of the world learning to play soccer was inculcated in players by their culture. That culture was permeated by soccer. Young players had many chances to make mistakes, try new tricks and learn the game while in player centered neighborhood games. These same youngsters watched professional and semi-professional matches in person or on TV regularly. They evolved into the game at a natural pace and moved into their first formal team at age 11 or 12.

And for generations those imbued with a love for the beautiful game learned the game from the game. Long before getting a spot on a team with a coach countless players had their passion for soccer deeply planted in the pick up games of their childhood. While the pick up game still exists around the world increasingly a youngster's soccer experience is centered on the formal training session and not the neighborhood game.

In the U.S.A. that soccer culture existed in only a small measure and almost exclusively in ethnic enclaves. For the majority of our players the soccer experience has been a formal one from the start. In that soccer background too much emphasis in the training of players has been placed on a robotic drill routine that has the coach at the center of the practice. Instead the game must be the centerpiece with players at the forefront of the action. Indeed both US Youth Soccer and U. S. Soccer have advocated a game-like approach to training session activities for over thirty years.

In "The Game is the Best Teacher" master coach Detlev Brüggemann puts this development approach into a style that you can use in your very next training session. The good sense approach of training players based on both an annual player development scheme and weekly match observation is presented throughout the book.

He looks at the game itself, takes situations that occur regularly for players and then breaks them down into a training approach that players of many ages can understand and enjoy. Even in formal training sessions coaches can use the game itself as the teacher of the game. Further the activities are such that coaches can easily conduct a most productive training session.

With the guidance of Coach Brueggemann you will come to a better understanding of the game and how to teach it to your players. Enjoy the Game!

Sam Snow
Director of Coaching Education
US Youth Soccer

1 INTRODUCTION TO A NEW TEACHING PHILOSOPHY

Training is defined as preparation for the game. This means essentially that what and how we do something in training should simulate the same actions in the game. Usually a player practices particular movements with or without the ball. This is to improve a particular skill or tactical movement in order to be more successful in a game, however, there are three aspects to be recognized which hinder a player from using in the match what he has practiced in training:

a *In training, a player often plays without the pressure of an opponent, time or the psychological pressure connected to losing a game.*

b *Drills and exercises are needed to improve a particular movement via more repetitions within a short period of time. However, the basic structure of many exercises does not repeat itself within a game. Those exercises might be well-constructed but they are not game-like. As a consequence, we recognize that the player does very well in training, but fails in the game when using the same trained movements. This is often because the player has practiced the particular technical or tactical movement itself but not the decision of when and how to use the movement as it is needed in a game.*

c *Training exercises often consist of just one situation in which a player can improve a particular technical or tactical movement. The drawback is that these exercises do not offer the connecting actions as they occur in the game. The player knows the requirements of the activity in advance, but ultimate success depends on the quality, timing and speed of the right decision in the realistic environment. During a game, these mental abilities are critically linked to and influence the players' actions. Anticipating how and when a particular situation will occur saves time and helps to assure a desired response. In other words, there is a big difference between a player knowing in advance (through a drill) that the ball will be crossed to him for a shot and that player needing to be aware of multiple options regarding how, when and where the same ball could be played.*

Game-related Training:
- an opponent delays as in a real game situation
- two teammates offer the ball carrier options for deciding how to procede
- game-like, connected actions required
- close situation, easy to analyze
- two small groups practicing

Past research points in the same direction. The speed and efficiency of transferring practiced movements and abilities into successful game behavior is significantly influenced by experiences which result from playing the game. These results have been confirmed by coaches working with these age groups. Children who have obtained quantities of game experience by playing not organized, small-sided soccer on their own were compared to those who did not partake in these activities. The same exercises were selected for both groups. The objective was to study the successful transfer of practiced movements into game behavior. It quickly became obvious that the experienced children showed much quicker and more efficient progress than those with less game experience. This strongly suggests that the fundamental learning level for sports like soccer should be game play, despite any lack of technical and tactical abilities and including all of its related mistakes and failures. This is learning by trial and error, by observing others and adapting their successful behaviors.

It's important to note that such a process requires significant time. To give some perspective, let us imagine putting together a puzzle. Is the one who finishes first the one who has seen the picture in its entirety beforehand or the one who has not? The answer leads us to the critical point of this aspect of practicing soccer.

Knowledge and experience about the use of a particular technical movement lead to a successful transfer of what has been practiced in training. Thus, technical and tactical actions should be exercised within the environment and situation as they occur in the game.

Considering what little time children today spend on playing soccer at school or in clubs due to the many other responsibilities and activities they have, the importance of the type and structure of exercises becomes obvious. Thus, exercises in which more than just one particular movement can be improved are needed.

TECHNICAL AND TACTICAL SKILLS SHOULD BE PRACTICED AS THEY OCCUR WITHIN GAME SITUATIONS IN THE REAL ENVIRONMENT

Such a concept is right on the edge of this new didactical soccer philosophy. Exercises should imitate typical game situations, even in a differentiated form, with regards to the players' level of knowledge and abilities. The player can improve a particular movement needed for solving a specific situation successfully, however he additionally learns to analyze that specific situation for the need and the kind of execution of the particular movement. He learns the tactical influence of his behavior on the actions and behaviors of the surrounding environment (the actions of the others). This means, in general, exercises connected to technical and tactical learning goals should not be constructed simply based on basic movements which are easy to be executed with the only option being multiple repetitions for the player, but rather suitable exercises should be extracted out of game situations.

To summarize these considerations, let's highlight three topics for efficient training, particularly with both younger and older youth players:

a The best training should refer to what is most suitable for the players' learning abilities, not just most suitable for the coaches' coaching abilities.

b The best exercises for players' improvement are those which immediately require players to demonstrate several abilities, just as needed in the game, even though it might be more difficult to coach the details within those exercises.

c Transition has to be recognized as a key ability for playing successfully in the game. This requires exercises which present options for both attackers and defenders, as found in small-sided games.

2 DEVELOPMENT OF BASIC SKILLS IS THE ROAD TO THE HIGHEST LEVEL

Players should practice what they need and how they need it in the game.

2.1 Times of Development

The manner, contents and methods of practicing depend on the age of the children. This is based on their current physiological and psychological development.

The first experiences for kids should be fun and to learn how to play with a ball.

A crucial distinction of how to practice with children during preschool, first and second grade is to **let them play** the way they want to and just observe what they learn about themselves (thinking and feelings) through the game.

Once children have gained their own experiences through playing soccer, the **systematical training** of technical and tactical movements can be initiated based on these first experiences. Systematical training means to explain, demonstrate and correct individually within topic-related exercises and small-sided games. Systematical training is characterized by analyzing **in detail**, correcting and complementing to improve **the precision** with which one plays, specifically in the area of technique.

Players' Development in Soccer

Fundamental Experiences
(5 to 8 years of age)
Getting familiar through playing
- gaining and processing basic experiences in human movement and games (agility, using a soccer ball)
- appreciating situations (space, speed)
- getting to know and becoming familiar with social attitudes (i.e. helpfulness, integrating, inspiring, leading, initiating, acting on one's own)
- improving decision-making abilities

Basic Training
(8 to 12 years of age)
Detailed, systematic training through activities
- stabilizing and further developing the abilities and basic movement experiences by appropriate learning opportunities and assistance (corrections, advice)
- improving precision and varied application of technique

Intermediate Training (I and II)
(12 to 16 years of age)
Developing and perfecting abilities under pressure
- perfecting coordinative abilities (agility), situation-conditioned use of soccer skills and tactical abilities under pressure (higher speed, smaller spaces, one or more opponents)
- developing and improving more complex game actions (this means training with a larger number of players – 5 vs. 5 through 11 vs. 11). Thus, more dependence on decision-making ability due to more complex opportunities for making own decisions
- tactical improvement through playing in larger spaces.

Advanced Training
(16 years and older)
Improving and stabilizing, in particular physical abilities

- stabilizing and perfecting tactical abilities of individuals, groups and the team against increasing fatigue
- improving and stabilizing tactics of attacking and defending as a team
- improving general physical abilities

Only when the players have learned to play the ball in a controlled manner during the game – this level should be reached by the beginning of puberty – can the exercises be extended into numerically larger training groups and modified through the aspect of **pressure**. Pressure in this sense means more opponents and less space, that is, less time for the individual to use his technical and tactical skills successfully.

The table on page 16 introduces the sequence of a child's biological development with the focus on how young players improve techniques, attitudes and abilities of playing soccer successfully.

There are some important aspects to this table of developmental soccer training. Each of the levels is characterized by certain critical objectives of training. These objectives need to be stabilized and improved to a higher extent within the next level as well, although this is not specifically mentioned in this table. The critical aspect at which a player is able to join the next higher level depends on the **controlled use of those abilities** which have been improved within the earlier level. That means if someone reaches an age characteristic of a higher level, but is still unable to play in a controlled manner under pressure, then he should remain practicing at the lower level. Thus, not the age itself but the level of player development has to be considered before joining the next higher level of training.

Training at the advanced level is described as being mainly focused on the physical aspects of soccer via special drills and exercises. However, this does not mean that during the lower levels of training there is no physical training at all. Physical abilities will be improved simultaneously within each exercise and small-sided game, in particular within exercises of longer sequences due to the game-related requirement to adapt.

2.2   Don't Train Against the Grain

Kids from four to about seven or eight years of age usually like to discover their own environment. In this part of human development, kids create their own games, boundaries and rules. They repeat what they have experienced in combination with their impressions in their own childlike manner.

Therefore, the typical expressions of a child's world should be respected as a natural process of development. Implementing drills according to adults' demands, in other words, systematic training in a too early stage of the players' biological development would mean to train against the grain. This can lead to a lack of development of the important process of self-identification within the social

Kids from 5 to 7 years of age usually do what adults want them to do even in training. But this is because they admire the father, the teacher or the coach as their role model, whom they want to please expecting his praise. So, they execute exercises as required. However, kids' nature is just to play. Kids need to play in order to digest what they discover and experience.

environment. Consequently such deficits could lead to problems with the development of one's personality and, in particular, one's social attitudes.

With regards to soccer exercises for the youngest ages; it is recognized that children must have fun engaging in drills and other exercises implemented by adults. This often leads people to assume that the children actually like to execute such tasks. However, they just like to please adults. This internal desire overrides their own intentions and preferences. The presumption that training systematically with preschool and first grade children would positively affect per-formance bears an opinion about efficient and successful training which is strongly against the grain.

> SYSTEMATICALLY TRAINING CHILDREN WHO ARE TOO YOUNG CAN HAMPER THE DEVELOPMENT OF THEIR INDIVIDUAL PERSONALITY

The years in which a child becomes familiar with the physical, mental and psychological conditions and briefly familiar with the game and the ball must be distinguished from the years in which human nature itself presents nearly optimal conditions for such development. This is the period from about 8 to 12 years of age. Due to the harmonic relation between body and muscles and an increasing inquisitiveness accompanied by non-critical encouragement, this period of development is often referred to as **the golden years of learning**. At this time, the biological development of a child offers suitable conditions for systematical training, even for difficult coordinative tasks.

Before this time of biological development, children should develop the motivation to play and to continue playing soccer for the years to come. Give them a ball and let them play. Observe in order to learn from the children's behavior. No demands, expectations, corrections nor interfering of any kind. It is still the kids' world. Let them discover it. Make motivation the key point for this game. Give kids opportunities to find their own options to engage in soccer.

2.3   The "Futsal" Ball Supports Self-confidence and Agility

Most scientists and experts in soccer represent the opinion that kids can and should already play soccer during preschool, all be it in their own typical way.

These are small-sided games with self-created rules related to the number of players and the actual environment. Beginners learn through imitation, trial and error. Such an introduction into the world of soccer provides foundational experiences in the technical, tactical, mental and, in particular, social components of this game (see table above). These basic experiences determine, to a high degree, the level of successful improvement of all abilities needed in the game throughout this period of physiological development. In short, the level of an adult's efficiency and performance depends on the quality of foundational experiences prior to the stage of detailed systematical training.

The developed physical, mental and psychological conditions of children from 8 to 12 years of age invite them to discover the game in the same way they observe adults. They slip into the role of their idols and imitate what they observe (even difficult movements) without any fear of failure.

Some experts, however, say that soccer can be played only after having developed technique with the ball. They refer to the difficulty of these techniques and point to the not organized way that kids play soccer. Indeed, kids' soccer looks more or less

like one dribbling with a bee swarm followed by kick and run. This is due to the basic problem of ball control, specifically, trying to play with a bouncing soccer ball. A small stone that wasn't seen on the ground can suddenly lead the ball into the air or in another direction than the player wanted it to go. Played too hard, the ball will miss its target, too soft, it does not reach it at all.

The most frequent problem a soccer ball causes for beginners is when it's played in the air and bounces along the ground. As soon as the player decides to get it under control, the ball bounces up again, too high for the player's foot to touch or to play it in the desired direction. The inexperienced player must wait until the ball comes down again to try to get it under control. This results in time for an opponent to challenge, or at least to disturb the attempt of the attacking player to control the ball. But even without being pressured by a defender, the time during which a falling soccer ball can be controlled is so short that even a skillful player must coordinate the speed and strength of his foot with the speed of the ball in order to get the ball under control.

> *"SOCCER IS JUST A MATTER OF*
> *SPACE AND TIME"*
> *(JOHAN CRUYFF)*
> **THE LEVEL OF PRACTICE REQUIRED IS**
> **DETERMINED BY THE AMOUNT OF PRESSURE**
> **FROM THE OPPONENT**

A beginner needs much more time for the same movement due to the lack of experience of how to time the movement of the foot with the movement of the ball. Children must do this in order to improve their coordination. One of these skills relates to an estimation of the speed of their own foot in relation to the movement of the ball and the speed of the ball falling down and bouncing up again. Research has proven that preschool children, when compared to adults, must compensate up to 30% for the inability to anticipate. This can often be observed when a ball rolls into the street and a child runs after it, even when they see an approaching car. The wrong estimation of the car's pace in comparison to that of the child sometimes results in an accident. Currently, improvement in skill and coordination seem to be preconditions for playing soccer.

This opinion is related to an already upgraded level of performance. But soccer can be played by everyone. The rules simply require one to play the ball with the foot or head into the opponents' goal. The methods and the styles of how this will be accomplished depend on the player's technical and tactical abilities as well as his game experience. Based on this, the "kick and run" style of beginners must be acknowledged as soccer...typical kids' soccer. This view seems to be of fundamental importance because just kicking a ball back and forth allows beginners to obtain valuable experiences through the appropriate and successful use of all the required abilities in soccer (as discussed above). So, the main problem for beginners remains in the characteristics of a soccer ball.

However, an appropriate opportunity which can minimize the problem does exist. Simply using another kind of ball leads children to a more controlled and self-governed style of playing soccer. This is based on an early understanding that soccer – with regard to the young ages in small games – is a game influenced by the ideas and creative movements of each player with the ball.

THE LOW BOUNCE OF THE FUTSAL BALL EASILY ALLOWS BEGINNERS TO HANDLE THE BALL SUCCESSFULLY IN THEIR OWN PLANNED WAY

To combat the problem of the bouncing soccer ball and a lack of technical controlling abilities we can use the ball of the game FUTSAL. The ball is smaller than the usual soccer ball and it hardly bounces. This ball is easy for beginners to control. This easier control encourages players not to just "kick" but to "play" with the ball intentionally.

Let's remember how a kid feels with a ball as his toy. When the child experiences the ball being easy to handle, he gets motivated to try all kinds of previously observed or self-created movements with it, to beat an opponent or to pass it in his intended way to the teammate. In many regions we can observe kids playing with found objects (i.e. small soda cans, knotted clothes) as an equivalent for a real ball. In short, the characteristics of the Futsal ball support the idea and understanding of playing soccer in a more self-determined manner. It motivates players to practice on their own at home or wherever space is available. This moment is the beginning of self-governed improvement in agility and fun in a creative manner to mimic movements with a ball. Furthermore, the Futsal ball also supports the development of risk-taking and self-confidence right from the beginning of one's soccer career.

To play Futsal does not lead to an increase in the technical level of the game of soccer. However, it does lead to an improvement of creativity with the ball. This supports the motivation of busying oneself individually with the ball.

Several people remark that the Futsal technique leads to a different feeling with the ball and therefore might hamper the learning process of "real" soccer skills later on. However, this is just an assumption. These people forget that many children in different countries do not have real soccer balls and play with all kinds of round materials: Knotted clothes, plastic bottles, even tennis balls or old and defective balls which also don't bounce. There are no indications of specific learning problems with these players as they transitioned to developing technique with the actual soccer ball. Rather, they obtained lots of game experience as well as additional progress in creativity by self-confident and conscious actions in order to influence situational development. And last but not least these players have made significant progress in comprehensively improving coordination.

Following these considerations, the smaller ball from Futsal should be used not only for competition but also for practicing as an appropriate aid to players during their first years of soccer.

2.4   Sample Drills for Kid's Fundamental Experiences

The following examples of useful games for children between five and seven years of age shall clarify the crucial difference among appropriate exercises used in teaching the basics.

"Tag"
- one marked field, 10 x 10 meters
- 6 players
- one player is "it" and has to "tag" another player by touching him
- if two players stand together they cannot be caught
- only a single player can be caught
- two players are not allowed to be together for more than five seconds
- a player who is caught becomes "it"
- he can be rescued by running toward the player in danger

"Dribble-Tag"
- one marked field, 10 x 10 meters
- six to eight players with one ball each
- all players dribble within the field
- one of the players is "it" and holds his ball in his hands and tries to tag another one by touching him
- when somebody is caught both players change roles

"Dribble-Goals"
- several small goals of two meters each - distributed randomly around a field
- the objective is to dribble through as many goals as possible
- no dribbling through the same goal twice
- players whose balls or bodies touch each other have to throw their balls above their head and let it touch the ground before continuing

"Dribble-Stop"
- one marked field, 10 x 10 meters
- six to eight players with one ball each
- one player is "the leader"
- players dribble within the field
- "the leader" will then stop his ball in a creative manner using his hand, foot, etc.
- all other players have to stop their balls in exactly the same manner
- the leader has to determine who was the last one to complete the task in the correct manner

- the last one has to then execute a predetermined consequence, after which he will become the next leader
- if the leader does not see who the last one was, he has to execute the consequence himself and appoint a new leader

Simple Small-sided Games
4 vs. 4 to two goals

Organization:
- two goals, 5 m wide, 2 m high, 20 meters opposite each other
- no marked touchlines!
- two teams of four players each in the field and one goalkeeper in each goal

Objective:
- play 4 vs. 4 to 2 goals
- playing time: 8 to 10 minutes

No variations.
No numerical changes.
Many repetitions in tournament form, framed through motivation to train coordination and agility.

3 PROPER EXERCISES TO IGNITE THE MOTIVATION TO PRACTICE

3.1 General Aspects

In general, there are three basic types of activities. All of them are needed in training, however, each for a different purpose.

- Small-sided games
- Complex exercises
- Simple drills

Each type of activity provides various learning opportunities based on specific characteristics. In order to determine which type is most appropriate for a particular training goal, we have to first analyze the main differences between each kind of exercise.

Small-sided games
- Two predetermined and distinguished teams (i.e. 2 vs. 2 on two goals)
- Specific rules regarding goal-scoring and restarts after a break in play
- Preestablished game duration

Complex exercises
- More than one player is involved in each movement
- Sequencing for a longer activity duration
- Connected actions as they occur in the game
- Improves decision making (players recognizing alternatives)
- Consideration of movements as required in a game
- Motivational for players
- Predetermined start and end

Simple exercises, drills
- Short actions
- Predetermined movements
- Predetermined start and finish of each repetition
- Selected technical, tactical or physical components
- Single or partner tasks

Each of these different activities has to be accepted as a suitable learning opportunity. However, when deciding which of them to implement in practice, there are two crucial aspects to be considered:

(1) The **duration** players can continuously exercise and (2) the **number of skills** which are being improved in addition to the specific learning goal of the activity.

For example, if two players play 1 vs. 1 between two goals for a specific amount of time in order to learn how to beat the opponent by a particular feint, then both players are given an environment to improve feinting. Additionally, however, both players will also train shooting, dribbling, recognition of the defending opponents' intentions, the direction and timing of when to beat the opponent and transition. Although this player would also improve their ability to perform a feint simply by dribbling towards and around a cone and shooting, passing the cone by executing the movement of the feint and scoring after having "beaten" the cone does not

present opportunities to improve tactical and physical abilities simultaneously, as the aforementioned exercise does.

Thus, it is the learning process achieved by each exercise that should be considered when preparing a training session. This can be done by comparing those abilities required by a particular exercise to those required in the game.

THE PLAYERS' OVERALL
IMPROVEMENT DEPENDS
ON PERFORMING EXERCISES THAT TRAIN
MANY ABILITIES SIMULTANEOUSLY

The following table lists the abilities needed for playing soccer successfully. The extent to which each ability can be improved determines the individual level of efficiency.

The abilities needed to play soccer successfully

Technical Abilities	*(skills with the ball)*
Tactical Knowledge	*(experiences)*
Tactical Abilities	*(reading the game, decision making)*
Physical Abilities	*(endurance, speed, power, agility)*
Psychological Abilities	*(risk taking, self-confidence)*
Mental Abilities	*(willpower, anticipation)*
Social Competencies	*(teamwork, sense of responsibility, helpfulness)*

Playing and turn-based soccer training does not just include improving technical, tactical or physical abilities. There are distinctive mental and psychological abilities to be considered as well, in particular, for youth soccer training.

Distinguished investigations within different areas of the science of human development have proven that sporting activities can have a remarkable impact on personal characteristics, social attitudes and health. The physical, mental and psychological abilities required for playing soccer successfully are mostly viewed in relation to the techniques, tactical and physical abilities needed for a successful and intensive soccer practice. However, the interdependence between the game itself and the process of learning personal characteristics and social behaviors such as self-confidence, responsibility to oneself and to society, playing within the rules, as well as helpfulness and teamwork must also be recognized.

Additionally, the technical requirements to control, play or move with the ball presents an outstanding opportunity to improve basic coordination abilities which are also needed in any other kind of sport as well as in daily life. These are, in particular, agility, flexibility, balance and adaptability within not organized situations.

Playing the game within small groups and small spaces provides the opportunity to simultaneously improve all relevant abilities for playing soccer successfully, as the game requires.

However, in soccer as in all other games these distinguished abilities depend on each other. This means they both limit and enhance performance. In other words, the different abilities should not be improved one after the other and then added together like singular components. On the contrary, it is crucial to improve them in the same manner as they work together in a game. This aspect is the background of the following statement, well known and acknowledged all over the world: **"Soccer can be learned best by playing soccer!"**

3.2   Constructing Appropriate Exercises

The general meaning of practice can be summarized as *"learning and improving skills and movements by repeating them within particular exercises in order to use them as successful behaviors in the game."*

However, to be able to execute skills and movements does not automatically mean to be able to play soccer successfully. Other very important abilities which the movements depend on have to be improved as well. The player must decide when and how he should use a technical or tactical movement in a particular situation. He must analyze the ongoing situation while playing to recognize the most successful way to get involved. This requires knowledge and experience already practiced in training.

Taken from this perspective, drills and simple exercises used solely to improve and stabilize the proper execution of a movement do not match the ability to use those movements successfully in a game.

Example: The skill of passing the ball
Exercise: Two players stand ten yards apart, facing each other, and pass a ball back and forth.

Such exercises are easy to observe and look well-organized. Because of the high repetition of passing the ball, the players clearly will improve their passing ability. However, this skill will be influenced to an even greater extent in game situations when the player has to decide whether to pass or dribble and when to do it. Failure in the game can still occur even when the player has frequently practiced the movement.
Consequently, more complex exercises should be utilized in which the player can learn and improve the movements used.

Example: Passing
Exercise: Four players try to keep possession of the ball against two defenders within a marked zone of 10 x 15 meters.

Many relevant soccer books today simply provide a long list of exercises for each of the technical and tactical movements of soccer as opposed to selecting different exercises according to the players' ability level and motivation.

Many of those exercises are constructed in order to give players opportunities to repeat a movement several times. Players practice the particular movement and decide when and how to use the movement according to the exercises' special situations. However, it can still be seen that even those players who seemed competent using the movement in training often fail during the game. This lack of success is potentially caused by the higher psychological pressure during games even though training game-like situations still requires pressure from the opponents. A more important reason for the obvious gap between successful practiced behavior in training and during a game must be identified as a lack of anticipating crucial situations. The player is still not able to foresee how a situation will develop until that moment in which he must demonstrate use of the selected

Finishing shows high risk-taking, willpower and the determined decision making to take advantage of each possibility to score despite the difficulty of execution and the lower degree of becoming successful.

movement in an appropriate and successful manner. In other words – the player will be surprised. This means he needs more time to analyze and decide what to do and how to do it. This amount of time is often not enough for a successful response.

Let's take common shooting training. Many exercises stick to just the skill of shooting with the right and left foot from different distances and angles. In the game, however, the player does not know in advance which position (inside or outside the penalty box) he can reach prior to shooting. This depends on the behavior of his teammates and opponents and can change during a game in many different ways. Additionally, one must consider that these changes in the situation gives the player no more than a few seconds to anticipate and decide how to act. Thus, the players who succeed will be those who have practiced shooting as following through with continuing situations as they usually occur in a game.

APPROPRIATE EXERCISES SHOULD CONSIST OF:
- **GAME-RELATED CONNECTED ACTIONS**
- **GAME-LIKE OPTIONS FOR DECISION MAKING**
- **GAME-LIKE ENVIRONMENT RELATED TO THE PLAYERS' LEVEL**

To summarize, the three aspects of training exercises in soccer are:

(i) Disconnected drills which do not link actions to a particular movement require more complex exercises to improve the game-like use of that movement. Considering the limited time players usually have for training, improvement via various kinds of exercises as well as increasing the level of requirements for each exercise according to the players individual progress needs a lot of work before the player is able to successfully transfer practiced behavior into game behavior.

(ii) Use of several different complex exercises does not automatically guarantee a higher level of improvement and, in turn, more successful game behavior.

(iii) Efficient exercises should include the connection of game-related actions and options that provide the player to decide how, when and with whom to act.

Considering these aspects, the evident conclusion should be that **exercises taken out of real game situations** can fit all of the aforementioned, advantageous experiences for the process of players' technical and tactical development. Additionally, the didactical line of selecting many different exercises for the same level of performance should be changed to a **longer duration of continuous training within one exercise and extending that exercise as the players progress.**

Throughout the following chapters, this didactical guideline and its pathways are described
- how a teacher and/or a coach can construct appropriate exercises for each level of efficiency by extracting desired movements and their possible options out of game situations
- how the situation can be varied according to the players' actual ability
- How an exercise can be constructed on the basis of the differentiated game-situation

3.3 How to Construct an Exercise Out of Real Game Situations

The topic to be improved shall be "Dribbling"

- We take a game situation in which the ball carrier is dribbling out of the midfield into the danger zone in front of the penalty box.
- We freeze the situation in front of the penalty box where the ball carrier has to decide how to continue according to the behavior of his supporting players and the defenders.

Counterattack against a not organized midfield:
One attacking midfielder approaching the shooting zone with two strikers defended by flat-back four.

To improve successful behavior of the attackers and the defenders, respectively, within this type of attack, the situation can be frozen and transferred into practice as an equivalent exercise based on this game situation.

Organization:
- 2 strikers and 4 midfielders vs. 4 defenders and 4 midfielders on 1 goal
- the attacking players defend 2 small counter goals, 3 m each
- 1 "keeper" defends each goal

Objective:
- After each goal scored, the next attack has to be started by the keeper of the attacking team with a pass to one of the a attackers, who must dribble first.

In order to determine if an exercise is equivalent to the actual level of the players, the game situation can be modified into an easier one, as needed. This includes even the easiest exercise for improving the skill of dribbling with the ball (level of six to ten years of age). The modification in this case concerns itself with the number of players involved around the ball carrier. This means one simple question must first be answered.

- Are the marking players in this real game situation needed for the ball carrier to improve his technical skill of dribbling?

These defending players can be taken out of the ball carrier's exercise to improve the technique of dribbling. However, they can be added later one after another according to the level of improvement demonstrated.

The four pursuing defensive midfielders are not needed for constructing an appropriate game-like exercise. They can be dropped out without changing the basic structure of the situation.

- What about the three supporting midfielders?

The three supporting midfielders are not necessarily needed in this exercise in order for the ball carrier to improve his dribbling. However, they can be added later one after another according to the level of improvement demonstrated

- Now, what about the striker in front?

Even the nearest striker in front is not needed for the ball carrier to improve his dribbling technique. However, he can be added later with regards to the learning progress of the ball carrier in order to construct a more complex exercise out of this particular game situation.

- What about the striker and his marking opponent at the right?

These two are not absolutely needed for the ball carrier to learn the technique of dribbling. However, with regards to learning progress they can be added later to the extent that the exercise continues to focus on the real-game situation.

- What about the right back and the inside left defender of the flat-back four?

Both defenders are not absolutely needed for the ball carrier to learn to dribble with the ball. However, they can be added later one by one according to the players' learning progress.

- And lastly, do we need the defender in order to make the exercise the easiest?

The easiest exercise to learn a particular technique (in this case running with the ball) should be executed without any kind of pressure. An opponent equals pressure and pressure increases the requirement of an activity. However, if the topic would be to play 1 vs. 1 to finish, then the opponent is definitely needed. In this case 1 vs. 1 would be the easiest game-related exercise.

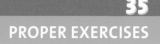

Each of the following exercises can be used independently of each other. Each requires a different level of experience and provides several options for successful execution of the chosen skill.

In order to find out the capacity for the player to improve a determined technical or tactical movement, the question about the players' experiences, skills and tactical abilities has to be answered. This answer guides the environment that is required in the exercise in order to enhance the learning process. The environment is made up by the players involved. The requirements of the exercise depends on their actions and specific responsibilities.

In the case of learning to dribble, children must first become familiar with the ball while running with it at various speeds, around obstacles, while changing directions, and so on. Thus, the easiest exercise for improving dribbling would be running with the ball without an opponent. Practicing without opponents lets children focus their attention on running and the moving ball. However, adding connected tasks like finishing requires children to notice their environment. This means learning to dribble, as it is required in the game, without always keeping their eyes on the ball.

Dribbling to a goal with a shot as a connected task is much more motivational for beginners, as opposed to dribbling around cones.

How can an exercise be organized in which a small group of players can practice dribbling to finish without long stops and starts?

Two small groups of three players in front of both sides of the penalty box The players of each group take turns. The goalkeeper throws the ball to the player, who controls the ball, dribbles and shoots.

3.4 Modifying Exercises According to the Level of Development

Once the players have improved controlled running with the ball at different speeds with sudden checking runs and changes in direction, the exercise can then be modified into a more complex one by adding options offered by this situation.

One of the options is to implement and increase the pressure on the practicing players. This happens when a defender tries to challenge and stop the ball carrier in front of the penalty box.

The ball carrier dribbles into a duel 1 vs. 1 against the defender to beat him and to finish.

1 vs. 1 on 1 goal

The opponent attacks the ball carrier as soon as the goalkeeper has thrown the ball to the waiting player. The dribbling player now has three options, (i) to beat the defender the defender with a move, (ii) to avoid to avoid the challenge by shooting from the distance or (iii) to run past with the defender with the ball. This decision depends on the defender's reaction. A second opponent defends against the other line's player.

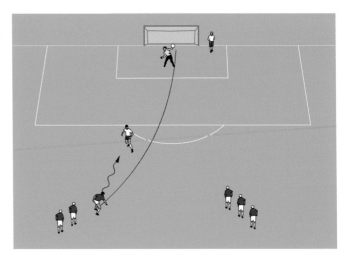

"What will happen if the defender wins the ball?"

After having won the ball, the defender can score as well by passing on the ground through the small counterattack goal.

Once having won the ball or by having passed it back to the goalkeeper, the defender counters together with his goalkeeper on the counterattack goal. He then switches roles with the attacker. This increases the motivation of the defending player to engage in a more game-like behavior.

1 vs. 1 with counter

To avoid the one vs. one situation, the ball carrier can get support from a teammate as it happens in the game. This modification of the exercise should be used once the players have improved the skill of dribbling and using moves as well as the risk-taking needed to win one-on-ones. The ability to win a one-on-one has to be understood as the most important ability when learning and improving all kinds of combinations between two or more players.

A player with an obvious lack of one vs. one skill would then not try to take on the defender when supported by a teammate. Such a player would only look to pass the ball to a teammate regardless of the other players' situation. Thus, it becomes easier to defend against him.

In finishing 2 vs. 1, the upcoming situation offers two options to the ball carrier:
(i) to beat the defender in 1 vs. 1 or
(ii) to pass the ball to the supporting player.

2 vs. 1 with counter

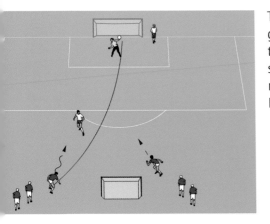

This exercise can be modified by combining both groups. After having controlled the ball played by the keeper, one player of the opposite group runs to support the ball carrier in a 2 vs. 1 situation. The next attack is then started by the other group. Defenders take turns.

After having learned and improved the basic kinds of combinations (give and go, overlap, takeover, crossover) within numerical majority situations (in this case 2 vs. 1), the pressure on the attackers can be increased by a second defender. The decision of how to support and when must now be made more quickly. This means basic supporting runs and options to solve the situation for the ball carrier should have already been practiced and improved.

Finishing 2 vs. 2 through the center: the ball carrier has the same options for deciding how to proceed as in the easier 2 vs. 1 exercise before, however, there is more pressure due to the second defender.

2 vs. 2 on 1 goal

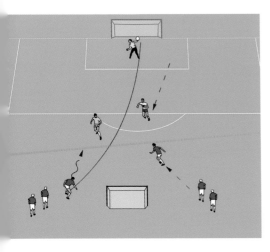

Now playing 2 vs. 2, both the ball carrier and the supporting attacker have to analyze the defenders' behavior in order to choose the most successful way of finishing against them. This means, the attackers must be familiar with patterns of different combinations due to less time and more pressure.

In general, to attack in numerical majority can be considered an easier task than to play against an equal number of defenders.

However, due to the more complex situation and the offside rule (which is another way to increase pressure in this situation), finishing with a numerical majority of 3 vs. 2 nevertheless means training at a higher level.

One striker is marked by one defender in front of the penalty area. The ball carrier dribbles toward the first defender and is additionally supported by another player coming out of the midfield.

3 vs. 2 on 1 goal

The striker in front can support the ball carrier by asking for a penetrating pass or wall-pass while the second midfielder advances to support, in this case in order to change the attack to the other side with a square pass. The ball carrier has to decide to go 1 vs. 1 or to use one of the different supporting options.

One striker at the penalty box marked by one defender. A ball carrying midfielder dribbles straight toward the box, which has now been taken over by a first and second defender. A third midfielder runs from behind to support the ball carrier and offer the option to change the attack to the other side of the defense.

3 vs. 3 on 1 goal

The second defender can cover his teammate pressuring the ball and close the space for a pass to the striker.

Thus, the ball carrier gets put under pressure. His options to continue the attack successfully now depend on the supporting moves of his teammates.

A fourth midfielder moves forward to support the attack. The covering defender now has to notice and perhaps mark him. Thus, the ball carrier's risk would lessen if he decides to go into a 1 vs. 1 situation. However, the midfielders should support on both sides and not just one so the ball carrier can change the attack to either side.

4 vs. 3 on 1 goal

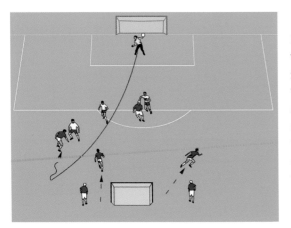

In addition to the options of combining with the striker, the third midfielder should support the ball carrier on the wing to create a majority 2 vs. 1 situation and avoid the 1 vs. 1 duel. If two defenders cover the space on this wing, the advantage of a majority on the ball can easily be created via a square pass to the other side.

As mentioned above, the situational pressure – as opposed to psychological pressure - is determined by the concepts of space and time. More opponents means less space, less space means less time to analyze, to decide what to do and to act in a controlled manner.

In this sense, playing against an equal number of defenders means less space to beat the defense and finish. The next exercise of four attackers vs. four defenders provides the same options as the last exercise of four attackers vs. three defenders. However, the space for executing those actions successfully has been decreased as a result of the fourth defender. The same methodological effect for improving technical and tactical topics can arise from narrowing the touch lines given in an exercise.

However, situational requirements constantly change due to the dynamic nature of the game. This means more defenders come into position between the ball and their own goal in order to delay and stop the opponents' attack. They had already been beaten but they immediately gave chase. The time the attacking players need to get into finishing position and shoot determines how many defenders should work together against the attack.

The following two modifications in the basic exercise for improving the topic of dribbling according to the chosen game situation show how exercises can be adjusted to a more game-like level. This is accomplished by increasing the pressure on the attacking players.

Two attackers play in front of the ball carrier and a supporting midfielder joins in against four defenders playing flat. The options the ball carrier has to continue the attack now rely on the behavior of the two strikers. The trailing midfielder supports by securing the attack.

4 vs. 4 on 1 goal

The addition of the second attacking forward and the fourth defender presents an exercise in which advanced objectives can be trained, i.e. the movements of two strikers against four defenders or playing against a flat-back four in general. Even this exercise is started with the long kick from the keeper to one of the midfielders at the small goal, so that dribbling remains the first action.

An important characteristic of the game can be layered into the exercise by using the factor of time to increase pressure. The number of opponents will be increased by a pursuing player. This challenges players to finish the attack faster. In this exercise the pursuing defender is allowed to start from behind the counterattack goal as soon as the ball has been controlled (this depends on the players' level of efficiency.

4 vs. 5 on 1 goal

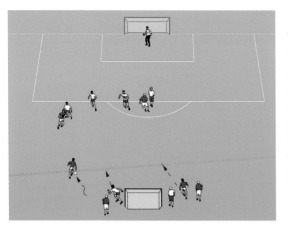

The addition of the second attacking forward and the fourth defender presents an exercise in which advanced objectives can be trained, i.e. the movements of two strikers against four defenders or playing against a flat-back four in general. Even this exercise is started with a long kick from the keeper to one of the midfielders at the small goal, so that dribbling remains the first action.

A second defender pursues in the next attack. Take turns.

Modifying an exercise in this manner allows the explanation of another basic concept of training real-game situations. That is to determine the position-related (functional) objectives of players.

An objective can be related to a particular position in the exercise itself or to a position in a specific system of play. When practicing with beginners or players of lower levels, the player will be told to imitate a particular game position, for example, the ball carrier from the first activities should act as an attacking midfielder. Here, the imagination of common and often-occurring game situations will be stimulated. Researchers in the field of learning theory have concluded that humans learn and retain best things which they simultaneously do and speak. Speaking to oneself is strongly based on the imagination of what one is currently doing. This can be observed in children's not organized small soccer games. They take over the role of their soccer idol and imitate, in a highly motivated fashion, how they picture that person playing in the same situation.

Tasks related to a position in a specific system should be used in training with players who are advanced up through the professional level. These types of exercises are described as "functional training." Training within the different systems comprises one of the vital parts of Volume 2 of the set Soccer Alive - The Game Is the Best Teacher.

The following three exercises show how to easily change objectives into position-related tasks for training systems.

Training a 3-5-2 system against a 4-4-2 system: In this modified activity, two strikers attack against four defenders to one goal. Three players build up the attack against two additional midfield defenders (in this case still recovering). Transition of the defending team on two small goals in the wings about 35 meters away from the goal line. Each player plays according to his position in the system. Position-related system behavior can be improved in detail as well.

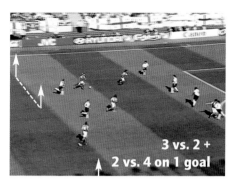

3 vs. 2 +
2 vs. 4 on 1 goal

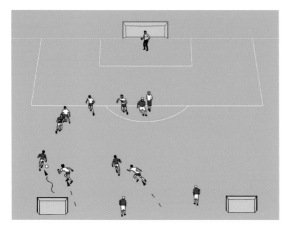

As long as the defensive midfielders' task is to pursue when the attack is started, the defense in the midfield is still not organized, thus it is easier to attack successfully.

Modifying the defensive midfielders' task to allow him to chase as soon as the ball is played by the keeper or even before would change the situation from counterattack to one against an organized defense. This results in less space to dribble.

Systems: 3-5-2 vs. 4-4-2 the offensive midelfield wingers are added. Now, five attackers are playing against 3 defenders in the midfield

5 vs. 3 + 2 vs. 4 on 1 goal

As soon as the ball carrier starts the attack, the midfielders on the wing can move to support until the attack is finished. The wing midfielders play two-touch.

The wing midfielders defend the counterattack goal when the ball is lost.

System training 3-5-2 vs. 4-4-2
We reduce the complete game of 11 vs. 11 into a game-like activity in which nearly all relevant behaviors can be improved related to the systems' positions. This is because we create more sitational-specific repetitions than would occur in a complete game. The fourth defensive midfielder will now be added

The exercise still stays with the counterattack situation.

However, now the fourth defensive midfielder pursues at the same moment as his other teammates in the midfield. The two-touch restriction remains for the wing-midfielders. Once the general attack has been improved, the two-touch restriction will be lifted.

As mentioned above, each of all the constructed exercises should be taken as a separate exercise. Which of these exercises is the most appropriate one depends on the quality and experience of the players. Each of the exercises provide different topics to be specifically improved. This means that, long-term, one exercise must be repeated in more than just one session. However, becoming familiar with the exercise's structure and requirements will become easier from practice to practice. This intensifies and accelerates the learning progress of game behavior.

Most of the technical and tactical movements in the game occur in more than just one situation. For example, long dribbling with the ball is also useful on the wings or in the depth of the midfield when space can be covered quickly by the ball carrier. Similar situations can be taken out of the game to construct equivalent exercises (see 6.2 Practicing in Game Situations, 1 vs. 1).

Game Situations

Dribbling 1 vs. 1 on the wing   *Dribbling 1 vs. 1 in the midfield*

3.5   Constructing Exercises for the Next Training Session

3.5.1   General Considerations

The coach observes his team playing in a match and practicing on the training field, respectively. In general, observations can be focused on two different aspects.

(i)   Due to the development of young players, the level and progress of their performance lead to that topic which should be improved within a systematic training process over months and years. This could be an extension of what the players have learned so far, sometimes additional options or new aspects of solving game situations successfully.

(ii)   The second aspect of observing players' behavior is focused on the actual performance of the players in respect to the team as a unit. This aim of observation is to check what has to be improved due to the upcoming match and, in particular, with a view of the next opponent.

Both aims of observation follow the same procedure. The coach analyzes the players' performance and selects topics to be improved within the next training sessions. In preparing each session, he recalls typical game situations in which this topic will be used successfully for achieving the desired outcome. This means either to finish an attack or to win the ball back in order to finish.

Situations as they occur in the game mostly require a lot of experience and abilities which adults and highly talented older youth players are able to perform. So, the coach has to adjust the recalled game situations down to the level of his players' performance ability, as shown before. This usually means to reduce the number of players, give more space and input particular restrictions or obligations without changing the structure of the situation itself. Tasks and targets must remain game-related.

We should train game behavior

- Game behavior is all actions (physical, mental and psychological) that are required due to the basic objective of the game and its rules.
- Game situations show objectives and options for the use of the game behavior to be improved.
- Exercises offer the opportunity to practice game behavior due to the players' level of performance. We do not train an exercise itself, we practice within the limits and options of an exercise. This means, the exercise provides only the environment and occasion in which different topics can be improved as they are required in the game.
- Rules, obligations and restrictions invite the players to use selected game behavior (technical, tactical, physical, social and psychological) within the game-related exercise (repetitions) in order to achieve the exercise's objective successfully.

Particular considerations have to be made when preparing the next practice session:

PREPARATION AND CONSTRUCTION OF EXERCISES
Didactical Considerations

Game observation:
- analysis of a topic to be improved
- analysis of game situations in which the topic (movement) is often used

Structure and form of the exercise's organization
- connected actions of the topic as occur in game
- constructing options for improving decision making and transition
- determining space and time related to the players' level of efficiency

Set-up in the course of the training session

In general, the different techniques of soccer should be learned without any pressure from the environment (including from the coach himself). However, as described above, all technical skills can be trained in a line of connected actions as the particular technique is applied to the game. The advantage for the easy transfer of trained actions into game behavior is maintained from the start and the motivation for practicing increases due to a longer training duration within one exercise. Additionally, motivation is maintained and increased because of the variety of different actions to be executed within one activity.

The following samples of the chapter show a game-related entry to improving soccer skills for beginners.

3.5.2 Technical Topics

Passing:
BASIC CONSIDERATIONS

- Level of the players: JUNIORS U12 years of age
- Game situations with space in midfield towards the opponents' goal
- Introducing the topic as an extended aspect of combining and finishing

Game situation:

Building up an attack in the midfield

Game situation reduced to the players' level

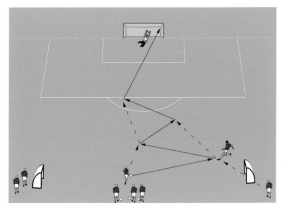

Organization:
One goal with two goalkeepers. Two small goals 3 m diagonal and 30 m opposite the large goal. Eight players, distributed into two pairs each behind one small goal, four players with one ball each in the center.

Objective:
One player runs through a small goal into the field to receive a ball passed by a player out of the center. The two play against the goalkeepers, who alternate turns.

Each player can take 3 touches (no dribbling) before passing. If the players succeed in continuously moving forward without stopping to get the pass, a scored goal counts twice. After scoring the players run back and change starting positions (switch lines). If the goalkeeper gets the ball, he can counter with a throw into one of the small goals which counts as one goal for the keepers. Competition is goalkeepers vs. players.

Heading:
BASIC CONSIDERATIONS
- Level of the players: JUNIORS U14 years of age
- Game situations with free kicks from the wings
- Introducing the topic as an extended aspect of finishing for the players

Game situation:

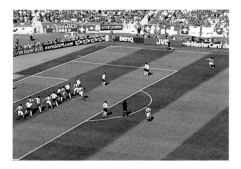

Free kick from the wing

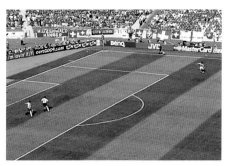

Game situation reduced to the players' level

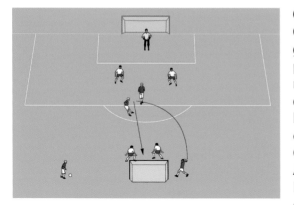

Organization:
One big goal with one goalkeeper. One goal 25 m opposite with two defending players in it. One marked heading line, 10 m opposite the smaller goal. Two defending players behind the line. Two headers on the line. Two servers each with one ball 5 m beside the heading goal.

Objective:
Alternately throw to one header on the line who heads to goal. The players in the goal defending as field players.

If the ball is defended inside the heading line, the two headers are free to attack and finish. If a server gets the defended ball back, he re-serves. If the ball is played over the heading line by the defending team, the other defenders in that half can attacking the big goal against the two headers, two vs. two. If the headers win the ball back, they pass to the server for another heading attack. After each goal, the ball starts with a new serve and heading attempt. Change the servers and the headers. Change the groups after about 24 total headers (six each).

Ball Control:
BASIC CONSIDERATIONS
- Level of the players: JUNIORS U12 years of age
- Game situations with space in midfield and on the wing
- Introducing the topic as an extended aspect of following through for the players

Game situation:

High defending kick to be received

Game situation reduced to the players' level

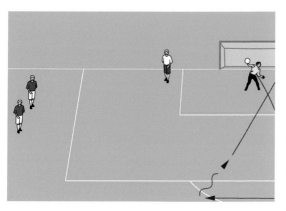

Organization:
One big goal with one keeper. One small, 3 m goal, 25 m opposite from the big goal. Six attackers, divided into two players each outside the box near the goal line (right and left) and two players at the small goal. Two defending players on the goal line beside the goal.

Objective:
Ball played by goalkeeper to one of the attackers at the small goal, who controls the ball, dribbles and passes to one of the supporting players on the wing. Winger controls the ball while the center attacker runs to support in the back half of the box (determined). Wingers pass to him. He controls and finishes. After each finish the attackers rotate clockwise and begin the next repetition on the other wing. Additionally, one of the players can run to defend as soon as the winger has received the ball. If that defender gets the ball, he can counter together with the second defender on the small goal. Change defenders after successfully countering with the attacking pair.

Dribbling and Feinting
BASIC CONSIDERATIONS
- Level of the players: JUNIORS U14 years of age
- Game situations with space in midfield towards the opponents' goal
- Introducing the topic as an extended aspect of following through for the players

Game situation:

Dribbling through the midfield

Game situation reduced to the players' level

Organized exercise related to the reduced game situation

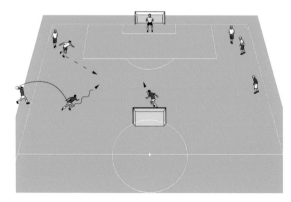

1st option:
Receiving the ball after throw-in from the touchline for finishing 1 vs. 1; practicing in turns on both sides

2nd option:
Teammate support from the middle, only one pass allowed, then the teammate must finish on his own; if teammate supports, his opponent marks him to challenge ball control.

3.5.3   Tactical Topics

Transition and fast counterattack
(coach a team to win the ball in the midfield/ in the defensive midfield for countering against a disorganized defensive formation)

Game situations related to this topic can be summarized as:
1. counter after ball won within a duel (1-1, 1-2)
2. counter after ball won by intercepting opponents' combinations

BASIC CONSIDERATIONS
- Level of the players: JUNIORS U14 years of age
- Game situations of winning the ball in the deep midfield
- Introducing the topic as a new aspect for players beginning within small groups step-by-step

1st step: winning the ball vs. the dribble
2nd step: winning the ball by intercepting opponents' pass.

Game situation:

Winning the ball in one's own half at the wing

Reduced game situation related to the players' level

First step: winning the ball vs. the ball carrier

In order to improve counterattack behavior in young players, drop out all those players who are not needed in midfield and defense.

We get the close situation around the ball 1 vs. 1 + 1, a supporting midfielder far away and 1 vs. 1 in attack (midfield circle). Due to the age and selected runs we reduce the space and organize an exercise related to this game situation.

Two groups train alternately to give the players time to recover after one attack due to the high intensity of such an exercise.

Organization:
- 1 small goal each 20 m behind the midfield line, 10 m inside the touchline
- 1 big goal with a keeper opposite on the box line
- two vs. one each defending one small goals each
- one vs. one each behind the midfield line in the other half
- one attacker each on the touchline with one ball
- two defending substitutes each behind the small goals
- one attacking substitute outside the touchline

Objective:
- practicing in turns on both sides of the big goal
- throw in to the attacker for finishing against the two defenders of the small goal; after having finished: next throw-in
- if defenders win the ball: counterattack together with their teammate in the opposite half of the big goal
- **restriction:** Only when the defenders win the ball can the throw-in player support his teammates against the counterattack
- after each counterattack, players are substituted

The next step combines both groups into one complex exercise.

Objective:
- If the defenders win the ball, they have the choice to counter on their own side or to switch over to their teammates on the other side for finishing together with them.
- throw in alternately from both sides

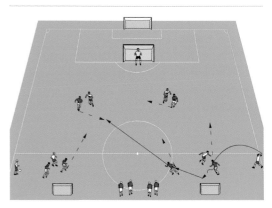

After progress:
Instead of throw-in from the touchline: pass out of the opposite half (view figure)

Second step: winning the ball by interfering opponents' passes

Game situations:

Intercepting opponent's penetrating pass in the defense

Penetrating pass into the space of a pushed-up defense

Complex exercise:
Organization:
- 2 big goals on each box line
- Two teams, divided into four vs. two in one half, 4 vs. 6 in the opposite half

Objective:
- attacking of one team after a long pass of their goalkeeper on the goal of the opposite half
- **restriction:** no back pass!
- when the ball has been won, the other team counterattacks

The special obligations present suitable opportunities for winning the ball to the team practicing the topic. Those obligations make it possible to perform more repetitions of the topic to be improved, "countering". Repetitions are necessary for the learning process.

Defending in flat-back four
BASIC CONSIDERATIONS
- Level of the players: JUNIORS U16 years of age
- Game situations of ball carrier approaching opponents' box
- Introducing the topic as an extended aspect for the players

Game situation:

Midfielder's break, facing own strikers

Game situation related to the players' experience level

First step:
Organized exercise:
Organization:
- 1 offensive midfielder and 2 strikers vs. 1 defensive midfielder and 4 defenders
- 1 goalkeeper in a big goal
- 5 m wide counter goal parallel to the goal line at the midfield circle

Objective:
- Offensive midfielder receives the goal kick and has to pass to his strikers for them to finish
- Offensive midfielder can support only from behind
- Ball won by defending players: transition with pass through the counter goal to teammate

Second step:
The offensive midfielder can play without any restrictions

Third step:
- another offensive midfielder is behind the counter goal in the circle
- the defensive midfielder can attack the goal kick
- in case of trouble, the offensive midfielder can pass the ball to his teammate and change positions to transfer the task to him

Counter goal

3.5.4 Combining Game-related Topics in Training Sessions

The practice time within a training session between warming up, the final match before the cooling down shouldn't be more than 60 minutes on average. One topic shouldn't be practiced more than 30 minutes in order to avoid complacency. A change of topic is needed in order to keep the players' motivation and concentration.

However, a heightened motivation and experience could be presented when exercises of different topics are combined into a final complex exercise as those situations occur in the game.

As an example, the lack of support given by strikers to midfielders who are in ball possession is chosen as a topic to be improved. Due to the higher intensity of the topic's requirements, the strikers' support will be practiced first

In order to construct an appropriate exercise for this topic, the same game situation as in the defending example above can be taken as background. In general, different topics can be improved in attack as well as in defense within most game situations. (In this example: dribbling for finishing under pressure; combinations of 2-2 or the defending of the inside defenders).

Strikers' support of ball-carrying midfielders
BASIC CONSIDERATIONS
- Level of the players: JUNIORS U14 years of age
- Game situations of ball carrier approaching opponents' box
- Introducing the topic as an extended aspect of combining for the players

Game situation:

Strikers ahead of ball carrier in midfield   *Game situation reduced to players' level*

Due to the strikers' lack of support to midfielders in ball possession, this exercise is focused in particular on the strikers' movements ahead of the ball-carrying midfielders for finishing through the center. This means the observation and corrections in this exercise have to be focused at first on the striker's supporting behavior.

Organization:
- 1 big goal with a goalkeeper
- 2 counter goals, 3 m wide, parallel to the sidelines, 35 m ahead of the goal and opposite to another
- 5 attackers at the middle circle, 2 defenders vs. 1 attacker in front of the penalty box

Objective:

- 1 midfielder tries to finish together with his striker in front of the box against 2 defenders
- If defenders win the ball: they counter by passing the ball through the counter goals and changing tasks with the attackers

Goalkeeper plays the ball to one of the attackers at the circle
The attacker controls the ball and goes for a goal supported by the striker in front.
The second topic could be chosen as a follow-up within a systematic training process lasting over a few weeks:

Keeping ball possession
BASIC CONSIDERATIONS
- Level of the players: JUNIORS U16 years of age
- Game situations of building up an attack in the own half
- Introducing the topic as an experienced aspect to be improved

Game situation:

Building up an attack from the defense   *Reduced situation related to the age of players*

Organization:

- 4 defenders and 1 defensive midfielder; 2 strikers and 1 offensive midfielder in one half
- 1 goalkeeper opposite at the box line
- 2 counterlines on the midfield line, 10 m each, 5 m inside the touchline

Objective:

- Defenders win the goalkeeper's kick against the attacking strikers, transit by dribbling over one counterline and pass back to the keeper
- The strikers and offensive midfielder try to win the ball and kick it into the undefended goal

Combining both topics into one final exercise:

Organization:

- Additional goal with keeper in the opposite half 25 m behind the midfield line
- 2 defenders vs. 1 striker

Objective:

- The midfielder finishes together with the striker after having passed the midfield line by dribbling 2 vs. 2
- If the defenders win the ball, they transition to pass to their teammates into the other half and follow to support
- The next exercise begins after each break because of ball "out of the field".

3.6   How to Construct a Small-sided Game

Sample 1

A particular topic has been observed to need improvement during the next training session. In this case let's say it's **"finishing quickly."**

Game situations are then selected in which this particular topic usually occurs.

Small-sided game: 3 vs. 3

Those players from this example who are not needed in order to train the topic in a small-sided game are removed so that two equal groups remain, in this case: **3 vs. 3 to one goal.**

The next step is to construct an option to transition. In this case: a 2nd goal with a goalkeeper on a line marked 35 m opposite to the other goal.

Small-sided game: 3 vs. 3 on two goals

3 vs. 3 is a very intensive game which can be played, in this case in a 35 m long field, for only about six minutes with full concentration. In order to extend the playing time relative to the length of a training session and therefore gain experience, each of the groups gets a 2nd group which changes continuously due to a special rule:

Each team divided into two groups of three, playing in turns. After each finish the defending groups change for the attack, the last attackers remain on the field to move (transition) to defense.

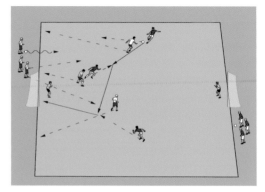

Sample 2:
Topic: "Wing attack"

Game situation:

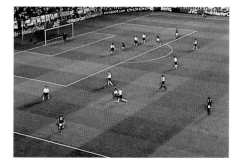

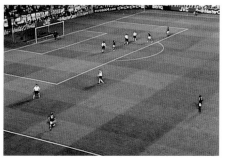

Wing attack　　　　　　　　　　*Related to players' level*

Organization:
- 1 big goal with neutral goalkeeper
- 2 counter lines, 10 m wide, 35 m opposite the big goal, 10 m inside each touchline;
- 2 teams with 5 players each:

Objective:
- 5 vs. 5 on one goal (4 defenders + 1 defensive midfielder vs. 2 strikers + 3 midfielder)
- each attack has to be started by passing to a winger and overlapping him, then free play
- goal scored and goal missed: ball is played by goalkeeper back to one of the players on the attacking team for its next attack;
- ball won by goalkeeper and defenders: counter on two lines
- defenders dribbling over one counter line: teams change tasks, defenders attack at once towards the big goal
- play time: 10 minutes

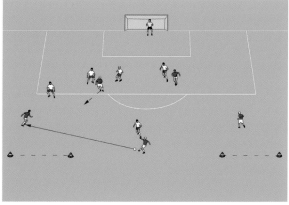

4 COACHING THE DETAILS ACCELERATES IMPROVEMENT

Activities are merely learning opportunities.
Corrections, demonstrations and detailed explanations allow for improvement and progress.

4.1 General Aspects

Coaching has to be considered an educational process. The coach explains and demonstrates to the players how they can act more successfully under particular circumstances and in specific situations. Coaching is strictly related to the basic scientific theories of the learning process.

Researchers have found that humans learn most efficiently not only by hearing but also by doing and additionally explaining their actions. This should be considered for coaching soccer as well. It underlines the importance of three basic aspects of training:

1 to first let players discover a new task
2 to provide exercises which offer the players the opportunity to find out appropriate solutions on their own
3 to encourage the players to communicate with each other

4.2 The Principle of Discovery

Children perform activities which they have created themselves with much more motivation and concentration. Therefore, they should be given a voice in setting up and organizing suitable exercises.

They should be encouraged to make their own proposals to be shortly discussed with the coach. When they feel their ideas are taken seriously, players' motivation increases to contribute in training and, in turn, to physical activity in a more responsible manner. The set- up for an exercise can be managed by the players themselves. Players can be entrusted to perform several particular tasks, or example to referee, to keep time or to draw up a list of the players having taken part in the practice or a list of specific results.

However, the highest motivation children and adolescents will reach is when they have the opportunity to play uninfluenced. This can be arranged in training sessions when, for example, the learning goal is to be improved within a small-sided game. The players' first experience is one based on discovery to achieve the learning goal. This means players learn first through the principle of "trial and error."

4.3   The Principle of Guiding and Developing Experience

The general aim of coaching soccer players should be to enable them to help themselves play more successfully in the game. Coaching means support and assistance to improve the player's ability to play successfully and independently from the orders and demands of the coach.

In this sense, the basic goal of coaching should be to show, to demonstrate and to explain successful behavior to the players as well as demonstrate why another movement or behavior will be more successful in a given situation. Showing reasons for more successful behavior not merely through words but also by demonstration lets the players realize the details of possible playing options.

Demonstrations and explanations should always be done in relation to the expected behavior of the opponents and one's teammates within a particular situation. The players can experience which behavior will be successful if the defenders act in a predictable manner. Explaining and demonstrating successful behavior is known as the **If – Then-principle.** It additionally improves the player's ability to make decisions.

Short explanations together with clear and fact related demonstrations open the players' minds and interest in corrective comments.

Decision making has to be considered one of the most important abilities in games like soccer. This ability requires one to analyze the current situation, to anticipate and foresee the intentions of the others (in particular the opponents) and to react faster and more successfully based on the others' expected actions.

The typical player's question should be **"why should I do that?"** The answer we sometimes hear on the field, **"because I am telling you,"** or **"because I am the coach"** does not make any sense in the learning process. The player has to be convinced of a suggested and demonstrated movement and behavior. The answer from the coach should be something like **"due to the movements of the other players, so why don't you try this?"**

Regarding the basic learning principle of guided discovery, there is no need to explain the features and details of executing technical movements or tactical behavior in advance. In contrast to this methodological way sometimes used and needed for training other kinds of sports, specific advice given previous to starting an exercise focuses the player's attention on the advice and hinders the gaining of important experiences resulting from guided discovery.

Coaching player movements and techniques needed in the game means supporting and developing experience and knowledge through demonstrations and corrections if player's mistakes and problems become obvious. Thus, interruptions of the training session present the most efficient opportunity to let players improve their technical and tactical abilities.

In order to correct and improve players' movements and behavior, the coach interrupts the ongoing practicing. Each player stays standing in the position he was in when the action was stopped. Thus, the current scenario gets "frozen". The players now have a look at the situation without any pressure. Frozen situations enable the coach to explain and demonstrate to a single or a group of players how to act more efficiently within a particular situation and why the demonstrated option will be more successful. The players can take time to observe and repeat the demonstrated actions for a better understanding. The situation is repeated without defense. This is followed by doing it again and the coach exactly indicating the moment when play is resumed.

The following two examples shall elaborate the principle of coaching in a training session. One example is related to a technical mistake. The second one relates to a tactical error.

Example: Technical error – shooting with the instep

The player (blue) diagonally right from the goal inside the box takes the risk to shoot the cross ball coming from the left wing volley with the right foot.

Instep:

Relevant technical coaching points:
- standing close **beside the ball** when kicking it

Even professional soccer players (like Figo) can sometimes fail during the game because of difficult soccer techniques.

The white lines show the level of the standing leg.
A shows that the ball played from the left side has already passed the level of the standing leg before the player strikes the ball. In **B** the position of the ball far to the side of the standing leg when the player strikes it can be recognized. Picture **C** shows the ball being hit not right *in the middle* but rather *off-center of the middle*. Also, one can see that the result is the ball spinning out of control Hitting the ball right or left of center puts a spin on the ball, therefore the ball cannot go into a straight direction as intended. The last picture **D** further demonstrates this error (bad luck). The ball flies high over the bar into the sky.

AFTER YOU SHOOT

ALWAYS ALWAYS!!

Advice for shooting with the instep:
Follow the shot in case of a rebound opportunity.

Key-point of execution:
To hit the ball close to (beside) the standing leg

FOR AN ACCURATE SHOT

WHEN SHOOTING

To correct such an error in training, the player should be removed from the ongoing activity while the others continue. Here, the coach (or another player) can separately demonstrate for him how to use the instep to shoot more successfully.

The dialog should lead the player to observe exactly which part of the movement he has to improve.

SHOOTING ACCURACY

"Observe my shot, do I contact the ball in front of my standing leg or right beside it?"

The player now concentrates on the observation of the crucial location of the point of contact. The demonstration should always show correct actions only. The ball must be hit closely beside the planted leg.

The player's answer usually points out the correct version. After having observed the correct execution of the movement, the player tries to repeat what he has observed. Finally, he joins the practice group again to continue the exercise.

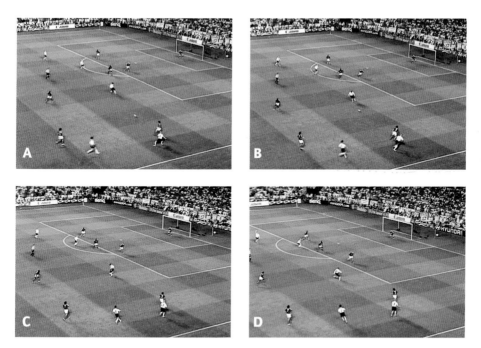

Example: Tactical error of the defenders

The striker (white shirt) runs to support his teammate on the wing to get the ball (A). Two inside defenders (blue shirts) are watching him move but nobody follows to challenge him to prevent the striker from turning and facing the defenders and the goal (B). The striker can easily turn (C) and challenge a single defender without cover at the top of the penalty box (D).

To correct this error in practice, the situation will be stopped at the moment the winger carries the ball. Each of the players remain standing in their positions when the play is stopped. In other words, the players get a "frozen" situation to be analyzed.

Principle of defending:
Always cover the most dangerous scoring options the attack has.

Solution:
The defender nearest to the supporting striker follows the striker and keeps him tightly marked. The right defender shifts inside to mark the other striker at the edge of the box. A long cross to the other side should be hindered by the defender pressuring the ball.

Other options in this particular situation, from the defenders' point of view, will be demonstrated in slow motion and explained from the perspective of why the demonstrated behavior will be more successful. The coach clearly indicates the more successful action when the play is fully live (100% all players are participating). The players rehearse the new option, followed by a restart of the game from a point prior to when the coach initially stopped it so that the desired behavior can again be practiced.

Corrections should only be made when an error has been repeated more than once or twice. The coach should correct individual players separately next to the training field. If, however, an error is made by several players, the correction should demonstrated in front of the whole group.

Only one error should be corrected in detail at a time in order to avoid confusion by the players. Again, only the successful execution of a specific movement should be demonstrated. Do not give examples of how not to do something.

Lead the player to the solution through precise questions regarding the correct movement. The player should then repeat the correction.

In general, only critical errors should be corrected, not every single minor mistake. Permanent interruptions in order to correct errors decrease player motivation. In this case corrections can be defined as those which directly support the specific action being trained.

The following table presents an overview of the general methodological considerations to be made in order to achieve the optimal training progression for players of all ages.

EXECUTION AND CORRECTION
Methodological considerations

Explanation of the task
- show the course of action
- precise and short explanation to the players or question
- clear demonstration of the sequence

Start of action
- observation of players executing the given task
- frequent execution
- time given for repetition and learning
- players find their own solutions
- players' modifications of the initial task accepted

Assessment of practice
- corrections
- adjustment to structure
- adjustment to number of players
- possible simplification of the task
- correction of individual and small group errors
- progression based on players' successful execution of previous task

✗COMMUNICATING WITH EACH OTHER

4.4 The Principle of Coaching Each Other

In addition to physical movement, support can also be given through communication to draw a teammate's attention to a special situation and perhaps give him advice. Such communication should be understood as assistance within a team in areas like space, covering or supporting runs. Such communication involves special words. They have to be understood by every player in a particular way. This means everyone should immediately understand what the calling player wants to express, for example:

1) *keep it*   means: keep control of the ball, there is no option to play right now, support is coming

2) *man on*   means: pay attention, an opponent is on your back

3) *one-touch*   means: play the ball immediately back to maintain ball possession, the defender is marking you tightly

REACTION SPEED

Players need time to observe and analyze the development of an ongoing situation in order to determine the most successful response. The quicker a player is able to respond, the less time the opponent is given to react. Therefore, reaction speed has to be considered one of the most important factors to play successfully. Talking while playing shortens the time needed to analyze and decide. Based on this, every player should consider himself the coach of his teammates both in front of and next to him. This is due to the fact that he can observe what occurs beyond his teammates' field *of view*

> "IN THE GAME EACH PLAYER MUST BE THE COACH OF HIS TEAMMATES IN FRONT OF AND TO THE SIDE OF HIM."
>
> (Johan Cruyff)

of vision. A player behind can guide those in front of him. This is most obvious in the case of the goalkeeper due to his position on the field. Thus, communication with each other in a predetermined manner must be viewed as important type of player support. However, players do not communicate just in an abundant verbal manner (mostly in defense) but primarily by sight and runs (mostly in attack).

In general supportive communication is based on game experiences, motivation and taking the risk to speak while playing. This topic should be improved and developed right from the start of one's soccer career through the use of specific exercises. Small-sided games and complex exercises developed out of real game situations are the most useful when it comes to training communication. This is due to their providing options for players to make decisions, sequencing movements as they occur in the game and extending the duration of ongoing training within those activities.

Players should be encouraged to talk while practicing and playing. They have to learn the difference between communication as support (an important social aspect of a team sport) and talk (noise, distractions). However, the worst action is calling for the ball when marked or in a disadvantageous position. This can be observed in particular in soccer games of unexperienced and young players. Additionally, players increase the sense of responsibility for each other and improve concentration on the game which then results in more efficient movements.

Being encouraged to coach one's teammates can improve the acceptance of and belief in the advice of the coach. Trusting what a coach or player has said increases the effort which subsequently follows. If there are any doubts in the players' mind about what could potentially result from taking someone's advice, then the players will not put full effort into it. Thus, doubt reduces success. Vice versa, the more effort a player gives in following a command, the better he will ultimately play.

Considering the principle of players' coaching each other, players should be invited and encouraged to talk during practice and games as it is an important means of developing their playing ability. The coach should request special leadership or organizational tasks be taken over by players. This is, of course, only after the coach has demonstrated how it is to be done.

4.5   Coaching Points, the Formula for Success

In general, soccer can be divided into three areas of responsibility for the players. As long as one team is **in possession of the ball**, each player on the team has to move and respond according to his positional responsibility, the current position of the ball and the tactical requirements to develop and finish an **attack**.

As soon as the **ball is lost** each player has to move and respond according to his position, to that of the ball and the tactical requirements for the team **to get back possession of the ball** in order to attack and score again. Thus, defending should be defined not only as preventing a goal but moreover as winning the ball back. Therefore, during the game the player must always be aware of his particular situation. This means the player has to analyze the situation and its options in order to continue. Specifically, he must continuously find tactical solutions and, once in possession of the ball, determine which technical movements will result in successful play.

However, the most critical area of responsibility is the moment of transition from attack to defense and from defense to attack. The faster the players are able to transition, the more successful they will be in attack and defense. This is because of the aspect of time for the opponents to organize their own defense and/or to build up and finish a successful attack. Here it becomes obvious that the ability to read the game and to make decisions has to be improved right from the start of one's playing career. The learning opportunities to improve these mental abilities, together with related attitudes such as risk-taking and self-confidence can be found in the coaching of an activity. The concept is simple and easy to understand:

In order to enable a player to transfer practiced actions into game actions:
* activities should include options to improve decision making, playing alternatives and possibilities for transition.
* the explanations, demonstrations and corrections should be detailed and related to real situations.

Coaching should not just be the repetition of common soccer phrases but rather explanations and demonstrations which are exact, detailed, and relate to the execution of a particular movement within a particular situation.

Therefore, in addition to the presentation of technical and tactical behavior in relation to an exercise, this book provides a detailed list of the most important coaching points.

Example: The topic is "Dribbling with the ball"

The important key movements to be improved: the player must govern his run with the ball; the ball should not govern the player's run
- dribbling slowly with the ball to shield the ball
- dribbling fast to get out of trouble or to use space
- using the inside of the foot to dribble the ball slowly and close to the body
- using the instep or outside of the foot to dribble faster (pushing the ball out in front)
- keeping the body (both feet) between the ball and opponent when shielding
- dribbling with the inside of the foot diagonally in front of one's body
- dribbling diagonally away from the body with the outside of the foot

The key points of execution focus on the use of the foot, body and head when receiving, dribbling and playing the ball.

Basically, the ball is played with four different parts of the foot.
1. the instep   2. the inside   3. the outside   4. the toe

Additionally, a ball in the air can be collected and controlled after first having been received with the **body (chest, leg)**. Sometimes the ball is played with the **heel** or the **sole** of the **foot**.

Regardless of whether a player is receiving, dribbling, passing or shooting, the key points for successful execution must be learned and improved upon. These key points relate to the plant leg and the kicking leg. The correct execution enables the controlled movement of the ball into the desired direction because of a well-balanced body.

Shooting

Coaching Points of Basic Soccer Skills
Using the instep:
Coaching points

Planted leg: • weight fully on the sole of the foot
• knee slightly bent

Kicking leg: • toe down
• ankle locked
• play the ball with the full instep
• play the ball close to the planted foot
• land on the kicking leg
• knee over the ball

Using the inside:
Coaching points

Planted leg:	• weight fully on the sole of the foot
	• knee slightly bent
Kicking foot:	• toe up
	• ankle locked
	• play the ball with the full inside of the foot

• kicking foot two to three inches off the ground
• bring kicking leg forward and up or across the planted leg
• play the ball close to the planted foot
• follow through in the direction the ball is to travel

Using the outside:
Coaching points

Planted leg:	• weight fully on the sole of the foot; at least one foot away from the ball
	• knee slightly bent
Kicking foot:	• toe parallel to the ground or pointed down
	• ankle fixed, tension in the foot
	• play the ball with the whole outside of the foot

• play the ball diagonally away from the planted leg

Using the head:
Coaching points

• play the ball with the forehead
• eyes open, face the ball prior to heading
• neck is stable and fixed
• power comes from the extension and flexion of the torso
• follow through with eyes open into the desired direction
• when jumping with both legs or with one leg out of a run, arrive early before the ball arrives and prepare the torso (extension)

Dribbling:
Coaching points
- dribble with the inside of the foot diagonally across the body; with the outside diagonally away from the body (feinting)

- dribble with the outside of the foot (for speed)
- dribble to the side of the opponent to force him to move sideways
- maintain speed and ball control when dribbling against a defender (don't lose time)
- entice defender by feinting, i.e. step to the side first

Receiving balls on the ground:
Coaching points
- move toward the ball
- slow down just before touching the ball
- keep body between ball and defender
- planted leg knee slightly bent
- control the ball one step from the body with the first touch

- "give" with the receiving foot when first contacting the ball
- first touch close to the planted leg (ball comes to foot)
- following the first touch in one motion, step in the direction of the ball

Receiving balls in the air:
Coaching points
with the foot:
- give with and move with the ball on the first touch
- don't let the ball bounce
- receive the ball with the foot turned in or out just before it hits the ground

with chest (on ground):
- both feet on the ground, knees slightly bent
- arch towards the ball, give with the first touch
- arms back, body stable (particularly when jumping to chest)
- knock the ball down

Shooting:

Coaching points

- shoot as soon as an opportunity presents itself
- shoot from the distance using the instep
- use the foot which is able to shoot the quickest
- observe the movement of the goalkeeper before shooting the ball
- follow the shot in case of a rebound
- shoot from close range using the inside of the foot
- challenge the goalkeeper by dribbling and feinting if he comes out

Basic Coaching Points of Defending

Delaying:

Coaching points

- cover the lane to the goal while delaying
- force the ball away from the goal
- move backwards to slow down the speed of the ball carrier
- keep one step away from defender
- watch the ball only, don't react to any body feint
- wait for attacker to decide on which side to pass the defender
- always be ready to take advantage of an attacker's mistake

Pressure (challenging the ball):

Coaching points

- challenge the ball immediately if the opponent tries to attack the covered side (don't open the covered side again)
- turn and challenge the ball as soon as an opponent plays it into the space behind the defender
- challenge the ball when running in the same direction as an opponent
- try to cross the path of the opponent and take the ball from the side
- use the body while running to the ball to further pressure the opponent away from the desired path
- play the ball out of the opponent's control when both reach the ball simultaneously

Slide tackling:

Coaching points

- tackle the ball before contacting the opponent
- tackle the ball with one leg
- tackle the ball from the side or, when running together, in the same direction
- play the ball out of the control and direction of the ball carrier
- slide into the path of the ball to stop and possibly keep possession of it
- play the ball with the instep or inside of the foot
- tackle the ball when the opponent can't reach it with his next touch
- tackle the ball when close to it

The description of the following exercises finishes with each of the different topics which can be improved by using the respective exercise. Related technical and tactical **coaching points** can be found, if needed, in the **Appendix**. They are provided in addition to the basic coaching points described above and marked as "additional coaching points" with a numbered link to the respective exercise of the practice chapter (5.2).

5 GAME-RELATED TRAINING FACILITATES THE TRANSFER OF ACTIVITIES INTO GAME BEHAVIOR

Appropriate activities, not the number of activities, leads to efficient learning and improvement of soccer skills and movements in the game

5.1 General Aspects

Appropriate and successful training does not mean offering many different activities and drills. Activities are just learning opportunities. Players must have enough time and options to improve their skills, mental and psychological abilities and tactical and social behavior. The coach analyzes problems and deficits, but also enhances special abilities to assist the players with increasing their level of efficiency. The coach must be "switched on" and ready to improvise at all times. Therefore, one-to-one implementation ("cookie cutter" approach) of training programs does not make any sense. Modifications and changes are often needed due to the players' progress. Furthermore, things like weather, field conditions and other unpredictable circumstances may require the coach to adapt a session as the situation requires.

When preparing a training session, the coach should consider the objectives and topics to be trained, appropriate exercises related to the topic and player's ability level and the amount of time allotted for each activity.

That's why this book does not present full training sessions and a huge array of technical/tactical drills and exercises. Strictly following the idea of constructing appropriate exercises out of real game situations, exercises for children and younger players are described here based on 1 vs. 1 through 3 vs. 3 situations with many game-related variations. Many coaching experts say that "if a player is able to play successfully within a 3 vs. 3 situation, then he is able to play soccer." Others mention the importance of winning 1 vs. 1 situations as the indicator for successful play, pointing out that the advantage of a numerical majority with the ball also helps determine this.

5.2   Practicing

Situations 1 vs. 1

5.2.1   Game Situations from
1 vs. 1 to 2 vs. 2

1 vs. 1
- Facing forward, through the center
- Facing forward, from the wings
- Facing forward, in the midfield
- With back to opponent

Game Situation: 1 vs. 1, Facing Forward Through the Center

Game situation

Diagram of the situation

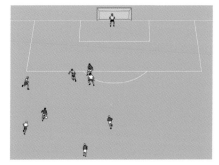

Appropriate exercise taken from the game situation
Level: The simplest task to improve 1 vs. 1 ability, Age: 10 years and older

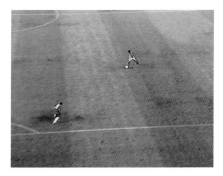

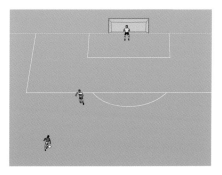

Organization of the exercise (1)
Organization:

- 1 big goal, 1 counter goal 5 m wide, 35 m opposite from the big goal;
- 1 goalkeeper with several balls;
- 10 players divided into 2 groups of 4 attackers each on both sides 30 m from the penalty box
- 2 defenders each outside of the box on both sides facing the attackers. Objective:
- Goalkeeper alternates throws/ rolls the ball to each group.
- Attacker dribbles 1 vs. 1 to the defender and tries to score.
- If ball is won by the defender, he scores into the counter goal and changes roles with the attacker.

In the following chapters different topics are added which can be improved within the described exercise. Thus, the details of an exercise don't have to be reinvented when training another topic. This simplifies the process of learning for the players.

To achieve this, particular key points of execution are described for each of the topics. They are summarized at the end of this book in the Appendix. The general keyword of a topic will be mentioned for more than just one exercise. However, the keypoints of execution always relate to the particular game situation and therefore are marked with the number of the particular exercise.

Topics to be improved (1):

In Attack	In Defense
Receiving balls in the air	Delaying
Dribbling	Winning the ball
Feinting	Tackling
Shooting	

Modifications to the exercise
in favor of the attackers
- the defender is permitted to challenge the ball outside of the penalty box only
- the defender is only permitted to block the path to the goal, not to challenge the ball
- the attacker can pass the ball back to another teammate when in trouble. The teammate then goes 1 vs. 1 against the same defender.

in favor of the defenders
- two defenders at the counter goal. One of them can pursue (chase) the ball carrier as soon as he controls the ball played from the goalkeeper
- a second defender can support (cover) his teammate as soon as he enters the 1 vs. 1 situation
- the ball carrier has to perform a specific move to beat the defender

In addition to each exercise, a small-sided game is also described in connection with the original exercise. These small-sided games can be used when introducing a new topic, leading to guided discovery as well as increased motivation. In this way, a coach can get a first impression of the progress made after going through the specific exercises.

The described variations of the session support the concept of differentiation according to the players' level of performance.

Small-sided game to improve 1 vs. 1 play

Organization:
- Two teams, four players each, two beside each goal, one in each goal and one each playing in the field.
- The goals are 25 m opposite each other.
- After each 1 vs. 1 ends, the player in the goal which was just played to dribbles toward the next defender while the next player moves into the goal.
- The players who have just come from the field return to the side of the goals.
- Playing time: 8 to 10 minutes.

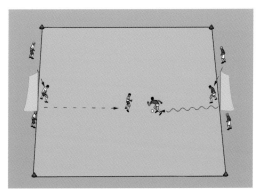

Variations of the small-sided game
- the ball carrier can play back to his teammate when in trouble. The teammate then attacks 1 vs. 1.
- after having scored, the scoring player remains in the field and defends against the next player of the attacking team
- another player of the attacking team can enter the field to support, but only with a one-touch shot.
- instead of two bigger goals, use two smaller 2 m goals parallel to each other either undefended or defended by one goalkeeper

Game Situation: 1 vs. 1 Facing Forward in the Midfield

Game situation   Diagram of the situation

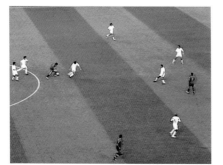

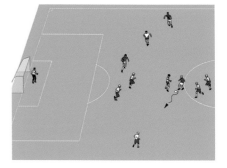

Appropriate exercise taken from the game situation
Level: The simplest task to improve 1 vs. 1 ability, Age: 10 years and older

Organization of the exercise (2)
Organization:

- 6 attackers in the center circle, 2 defenders at the edges of the penalty box
- The goalkeeper plays the ball to the attackers, one of them takes it and dribbles towards the goal while the previous attacker moves back toward his group and plays with the new attacker
- one defender moves to pick up the ball carrier, while the second one covers the supporting attacker
- the ball carrier can attack alone or play the ball to his teammate (one pass only) if defenders win the ball they counter to the counter goals, 35 m from the goal and switch roles, if succesful.

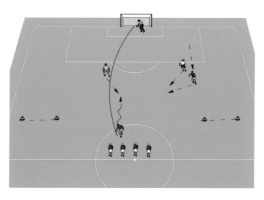

Additional topics to be improved (2):

In Attack	In Defense
Dribbling	Marking
Supporting	Delaying

Modifications to the exercise
in favor of the attacker

- instead of the second attacker and the big goal, two smaller goals of 3 m on the corners of the penalty area can be used
- when having difficulty controlling a high ball due to the pressuring defender, provide an option to play the ball to a new attacker in the center circle (change roles)
- the opponent may only defend up to a marked line, 30 m from the goal
- play without a goalkeeper (encourages dribbling into space and shooting from distance)

in favor of the defender

- the second attacker must play two-touch (pass to him only when he can shoot)
- additional time rule: after having controlled the ball, a shot must be taken within 10 seconds
- use the offside rule
- the second attacker (the first attacker from the previous repetition) can support only inside the penalty box, but the second defender can defend anywhere

Small-sided game
Organization:
- 4 small cone goals, 3 m wide, two parallel to each other, 15 m apart. The other two 10 m across from the first two.
- 2 teams of 5 players each; distributed
- 3 vs. 3 in the field between the goal and 1 each behind the goal lines.

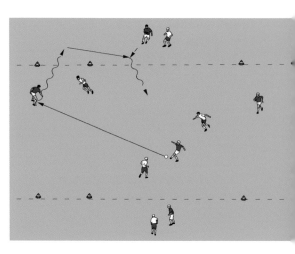

Objective:
- 3 vs. 3 inside the goals.
- Dribbling through a goal = 1 point, then pass to the teammate behind the goal line, and switch roles.
- The one who gets the ball dribbles into the field
- Playing time: 6 to 8 minutes

Variations of the small-sided game
- instead of two goals each, 1 marked line 20 m to be dribbled over
- Restriction: two touches to control ball before passing
- Another goal placed 15 m behind the line of 2 goals, which is shot on after having dribbled through the first goal. The defender plays as a keeper and attacks after a goal has been scored
- the defending player behind the goals can defend on the line of the two goals

Game Situation: 1 vs. 1 on the Wings

Game situation	Diagram of the situation

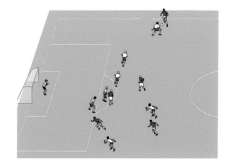

Appropriate exercise taken from the game situation
Level: The simplest task to improve 1 vs. 1 ability, Age: 10 years and older

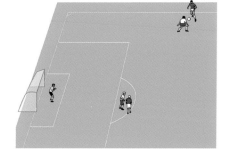

Organization of the exercise (3)
Organization:
- 1 counter goal, 10 m wide, 30 m opposite the big goal
- 1 goalkeeper in the big goal, 1 midfielder with some balls in front of the counter goal
- 2 players each on both wings
- 1 striker at the penalty box vs. 1 defender
- 1 defender each on both corners of the box

Objective:
- play 1 vs. 1 on the wing after having received the ball from the midfielder
- when having beaten the defender, 1st attacker plays across into the center to the striker
- the midfielder can then support the striker
- after a dead ball, the goalkeeper throws the ball
- to the midfielder
- if the defender wins the ball, he counters on the counter goal and players switch roles

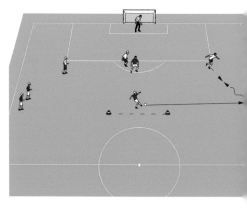

Additional topics to be improved (3):

In Attack	In Defense
Heading	Man marking
Dribbling	
Receiving	
Crossing	
Finishing	

Modifications to the exercise

In favor of the attacker
- the striker or midfielder can support the ball carrier with one-touch only to beat the opponent
- the attack can be switched to the other wing if needed
- the second player on the same wing can support the ball carrier by overlapping, etc.
- the supporting striker can feint and continue on his own when getting the ball

In favor of the defender
- the defenders can support each other
- defenders can use the offside rule
- no assistance from the midfielder
- time restriction: must finish within 15 second after the wing player's first touch

Small-sided game
Organization:
- 2 goals 30 m opposite from each other
- two teams of three players each, 1 striker in the attacking half, two players in the defending half
- the field divided in half with two marked lines, 5 m each from the touchlines

Objective:
- the strikers play 1 vs. 1 after having received the ball over one line.
- one player defends, the other one has to play in their own goal
- after having won the ball or after a goal/out of bounds, the defender and the player in the goal start their attack with a pass to the striker over one of the lines
- Playing time: 6 minutes

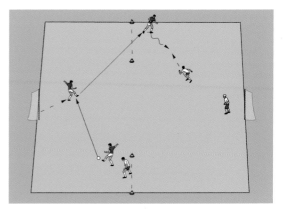

Variations of the small-sided game
- time rule: 8 seconds to finish after receiving the ball
- can't win the ball back after having lost it in 1 vs. 1
- play 2 vs. 2 in your own half. After having passed the ball over one line to the striker, the defender of the goal moves out of the goal to defend while the other defender runs back into the goal. The player who passed the ball runs into the other half as soon as possession is lost.
- same as above, however, the passing player follows immediately to support the striker, but with one touch only.

Game Situation: 1 vs. 1 Back to the Goal

Game situation   Diagram of the situation

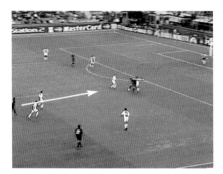   

Appropriate exercise taken from the game situation
Level: The simplest task to improve the 1 vs. 1 ability, Age: 12 years and older

Organization of the exercise (4)
Organization:

- 3 strikers with 3 defenders, 1 pair in front of the penalty box, the other 2 on each side of the box
- 2 midfielders against 1 defensive midfielder in the center circle

Objective:
- one of the midfielders, after having controlled a goal kick from the goalkeeper, passes the ball to the striker in front of the box, who takes on the defender.
- if the defender wins the ball, he plays to his midfielder, who tries to dribble over the half way line = goal. The attacking midfielder starts the next attack.
- next attack: a different striker asks for the ball while the last two return to their positions.

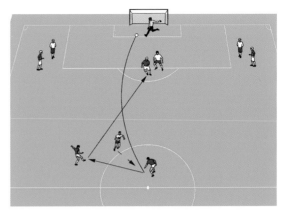

Additional topics to be improved (4):

In Attack	In Defense
Dribbling	Man marking
Receiving	Transition
Supporting	
Transition	

Modifications to the exercise
In favor of the attack
- the striker can play the ball back to the supporting midfielder and check off the defender to ask for the ball again
- the defender may not intercept the first pass
- the attacker can play the ball back to the supporting midfielders for a shot from distance
- the attacker can create space for himself and get a penetrating pass which beats the defender

In favor of the defense
- the defending midfielder can support his teammate against the striker
- one of the defenders from outside the penalty box can support the central defender
- the attack must be initiated with a long, high ball
- the attacking midfielder plays with two touches only (easier to anticipate when the ball will be passed)

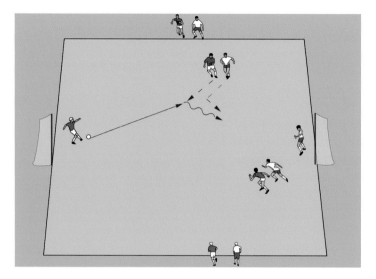

Small-sided game
Organization:
- two big goals 30 m opposite from each other marked field of 20 x 30 m
- two teams of five players each, distributed in two pairs 1 vs. 1 in the field and two pairs outside of each touchline, one player each in one goal

Objective:
- Each player can play against his opponent only
- pass from player in the goal to one of his four teammates, who tries to finish
- the player in the goal can support but not shoot
- on a turnover, all players of the defending team counter the other goal
- next attack starts from goal last scored playing time: 10 minutes (rotate pairs' positioning)

Variations of the small-sided game

- player with ball can be supported, but supporting player may not finish
- the player in goal has two touches only
- the substitute players outside can support with one touch only
- time limit before shooting

Developing Further Options for the Game Situation

Exercises can being expanded with further options depending on the player's development regarding the game situation chosen for practicing. This means, the structure of exercises do not have to be changed, rather the pressure on the players can be incrementally increased to the real game situation. Pressure in this sense should be understood in the following manner:

- more players (more complex exercises)

- less space

- more options (increase need to make decisions)

- less time to respond

Development of an exercise step-by-step should be based on the general game situation. The exercises become more complex by involving more attackers and defenders. This leads to more options for each player. The players will further improve the basic technical and tactical objectives trained in the more simple exercise. They now get to see and learn additional tactical options for solving the current problem. The advantage is that the players can improve their abilities and performance within a well-known environment. This results in self-confidence and motivation, both of which are crucial to the learning process.

The following examples show how an exercise can be developed incrementally up through the next complex situation to be trained: 2 vs. 2.

Game Situation: 1 + 1 vs. 1

The new component of this already trained situation will be developed with a second attacker.

The second defender at first will be left out of the exercise. Thus, all options of using the supporting teammate can be learned and improved as additional possibilities when playing 1 vs. 1 (1 + 1 vs. 1).

Organization of the exercise (5)
Organization:

- 1 large goal, 1 counter goal (5 m wide), 35 m opposite the large goal.
- 1 goalkeeper with several balls;
- 10 players divided into 2 groups of 4 attackers each on both sides of the penalty box, 30 m apart.
- One defender on each side of the penalty box.

Objective:

- Goalkeeper throws the ball to an attacker in one group, who dribbles 1 vs. 1 against the defender and tries to finish.
- The next attacker of the other group comes to support (2 vs. 1), however with one pass only. Once the supporting attacker has been used, he much then go 1 vs. 1 and finish. No further combinations.
- The defender scores in the counter goal, if having won the ball, and switches roles with the attacker.

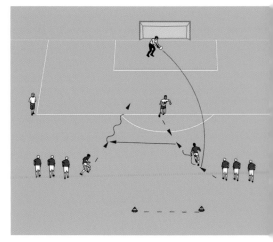

Additional topics to be improved:

In Attack	In Defense
Supporting	Defending against a numerical majority

Modifications to the exercise

in favor of the attacker
- the attacker can pass the ball to another one in his group if he gets in trouble against the defender. The new attacker then goes 1 vs. 1
- the defending player can only challenge once the attacking player starts dribbling
- the goalkeeper can play to the attacker who is in a better position rather than alternating groups
- the goalkeeper has to play the ball to the attacker on the ground

in favor of the defender
- time rule: after 10 seconds the second defender can support his teammate, making it 1 vs. 2
- the attacker has to perform a given move to beat the defender
- the ball carrier can only shoot inside the penalty box
- the second attacker can only support with two-touches and a shot

Small-sided game
Organization:
- Two goals 25 m opposite each other
- 4 players, divided into two teams, 2 vs. 2

Objective:
- play 1 vs. 1 + 1
- the ball carrier can be supported by his teammate.
- if teammate gets the ball, he has to finish 1 vs. 1 without any further support
- the second defender plays in the goal
- playing time: 5 minutes

Variations of the small-sided game
- time rule: finish within 10 seconds
- play to two small goals, 10 m next to each other
- the second attacker can only support behind the ball
- use substitutes behind the goals who change after each goal

Game Situation: 2 vs. 1

Organization of the exercise (6)
Organization:
- Same as above

Objective:
- Same as above, however attacking players may now combine freely.

Additional topics to be improved:

In Attack	In Defense
Wall passing	Defending against a numerical majority
Crossover runs	
Overlapping	
Takeovers	

Modifications to the exercise
in favor of the attacker
- the defender can start to challenge only after the attacker has controlled the ball
- pass on the ground from the goalkeeper to start the exercise
- no tackling against the ball by the defender
- the defender can defend outside of the box only

in favor of the defender
- time rule: finish within 10 seconds after having controlled the ball
- the second attacker can support, two touches only
- a given combination (i.e. give and go, overlap, takeover) has to be performed first
- two counter goals; the second defender can support the counter attack

Small-sided game
Organization:
- 2 goals 25 m opposite each other;
- 3 teams of 2 players each

Objective:
- attack 2 vs. 1 to 1 goal, the 2nd defender has to play in the goal as keeper.
- The 3rd team waits at the opposite goal.
- A goal can be scored after any kind of position change of the attacker, after each finish and turnover. The attacking team comes off and waits at the goal line. The defenders attack against the 3rd team at the opposite goal.
- Playing time: 6 minutes.

Variations of the small-sided game

- a specific combination must first be performed (crossover run with penetrating pass)
- time rule: finish within 10 seconds
- marked midfield line: the 3rd team can wait and defend at the midfield line
- marked midfield line: after each attempt at goal or loss of possession, the last attacking team can defend with one player up to midfield, while the 2nd player moves into the goal

Game Situation: 2 vs. 1 Increasing Pressure

Same as the exercise above, only each attack must be finished within 10 seconds

Having improved the basic kinds of combinations with the supporting player, the second defender now increases the pressure on the attackers until the real game situation of 2 vs. 2 occurs without any problems.

Game Situation: 2 vs. 2

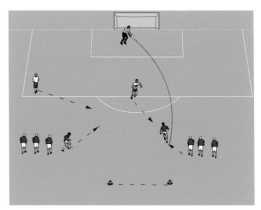

Organization of the exercise (7)
Next Progression:
- Same as exercise above, however the second defender can now support his teammate (2 vs. 2)

Modifications to the exercise
in favor of the attackers
- the second defender can only mark and play against the second attacker (man marking)
- when in trouble, the ball carrier can play the ball back to another player of his to keep possession. He then switches roles with the new attacker.
- the defender can only challenge an attacker with his back to the goal. No frontal challenges.
- other players of both groups can defend against a counterattack by the defending pair.

in favor of the defenders
- two players pursue the defender at the counter goal. As soon as the ball is won by an attacker one of the defenders heads back to defend with the other two.
- The defenders can mark an attacker when the keeper plays the ball, however, another attacker may receive the ball and start the attack.
- both defenders can cover the space in front of the goal from the beginning of the exercise up through 1 vs. 2.
- the goalkeeper may randomly play a goal kick at the counter goal in order to score. The attackers have to prevent the goal, win the ball and attack with two players against one defender.

The following samples are based on the general situation of 2 vs. 2. However, they present a particular moment and related progressions of these situations in which the duel 1 vs. 1 is just one option for the attacker to beat the opponent. The other option is to combinate with the teammate 2 vs. 2.

Samples of related small sided games can be taken out of the chapter regarding 2 vs. 2.

Game situation 1 vs. 1 + 1 vs. 1 on the wing

Game situation

Organization of the exercise (8)

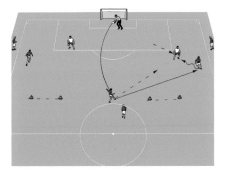

Organization:
- 1 large goal with goalkeeper, 2 small counter goals 35 m opposite the large goal, 2 m wide, 15 m apart
- 10 players, divided into 1 attacker vs. 1 defender on each wing and 2 midfielders vs. 2 midfielders in the center
- Defenders position themselves between the counter goals

Objective:
- After having controlled goalkeeper's pass, the central midfielder plays to one of the attackers on the wing who goes 1 vs. 1 to goal.
- After each repetition, the wingers and the central midfielders switch roles with their substitutes in position.
- If the keeper or a defender wins the ball, they counterattack on one of the counter goals. The central midfielder can support the winger's attack.

Modifications to the exercise
in favor of the attackers
- the defender can only challenge once the attacker has controlled the ball
- the central midfielder can support the ball carrier to beat the opponent (two-touch)
- the attacker of the opposite wing can run into the box and attack
- the winger can pass the ball to his substitute and switch roles when in trouble

in favor of the defenders
- the defenders can support each other
- the central attacker may not support the winger with the ball, but must remain in the penalty area
- the second central defender can pursue as soon as the ball has been played to the wing
- the central defender can defend in the wings

Game situation	Organization of the exercise (9)
	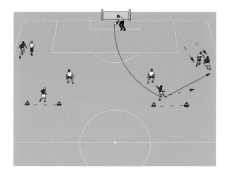

Organization:
- 1 large goal with goalkeeper, 2 small counter goals 35 m opposite the large goal, 30 m apart
- 8 players, divided into 4 pairs, attacker vs. defender, 2 placed at the wings and 2 in front of the counter goals

Objective:
- the defenders on the wings mark the attackers, those in the midfield covering the space around the penalty area
- alternating long throws from the goalkeeper to one of the midfield attackers to start the exercise

- the midfielder plays ball to his teammate on the wing who goes 1 vs. 1 towards the goal
- the midfielder can support the ball carrier until the ball is dead
- if a defender wins the ball, he counterattacks on either counter goal
- when countering, all players may get involved

Modifications to the exercise
in favor of the attackers
- the defender can challenge only after the attacker has controlled the ball and faces his opponent
- the midfield opponent can only defend outside of the penalty area
- the second midfield attacker can also support the ball
- the attack can be switched to the other wing when loss of possession is about to happen

in favor of the defenders
- the far midfield defender can defend with his teammates
- the midfield attacker must play two-touch
- the midfield attacker must play a specific combination
- defenders can defend together, however, the attackers must remain in their positions

Game Situation: 1 vs. 1 + 1 vs. 1 Through the Center

Game situation   Organization of the exercise (10)

   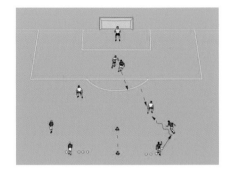

Organization:
- 1 big goal with goalkeeper; 1 small counter goal, 3 m, set vertically to field, 35 m opposite the big goal; 8 players, divided into 3 x 1 vs. 1 pairs and 2 substitutes behind the counter goal with several balls

Objective:
- 1 striker vs. 1 defender inside the box
- the defending midfielders cover the space in front of the box first
- after having received the pass from his substitute, one of the midfielders starts the attack towards the goal, the striker in front plays with him
- if a defender wins the ball, he attacks the counter goal
- the counter goal can be defended by the substitutes
- after each finish, midfielders change with their substitutes

Modifications to the exercise
in favor of the attackers
- the opponents in the midfield can only challenge after the ball has been controlled by a midfielder
- the attacking midfielder can change the point of attack by passing the ball to the second midfielder
- the striker can change the point of attack by passing the ball back to the supporting second midfielder
- the midfielders can switch roles with the substitutes by passing the ball back if in trouble

in favor of the defenders
- the midfield defenders can mark their opponents before the ball is put in play
- the second midfield defender can challenge the ball
- the midfield attacker has to start the attack by passing to the striker after having received the ball
- add to recovering defenders behind the counter goal, who alternately pursuing after attack has been begun

Small-sided game related to 2 vs. 1 progression
Organization:
- Two teams, 4 players each, two beside the goals, one each in the goals and 1 in the field playing 1 vs. 1.
- Goals 25 m opposite each other.

Objective:
- After an attack, the player in the attacked goal dribbles against the defender from the other goal while the next player from the goal line moves into the goal

- the dribbler and his defender return to their respective goals
- the 3rd player of the attacking team creates a 2 vs. 1 situation
- Playing time: 8 to 10 minutes.

Variations of the small-sided game
- specify a particular run or dribble to start each repetition
- the ball carrier can switch roles and positions with his teammate in the goal via a back pass if he gets in trouble
- the supporting player plays two-touch
- the 3rd attacker can leave the goal to support with a one-touch shot only

Small-sided game to improve progressions to 2 vs. 2
Next progression:
- Play 2 vs. 2 in the field.
- After a goal the two attackers remain in the field as defenders, the goalkeeper and one of his defenders attack, the other defender moves into goal.

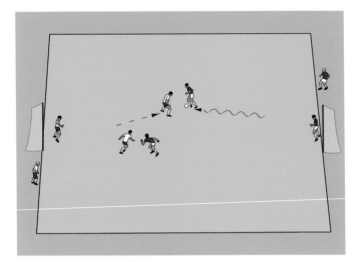

Variations of the small-sided game
- the attacker without the ball must play two-touch
- time restriction: finish within 10 seconds
- the players in the goal can come out and support in the field as well
- when in trouble, the ball carrier can switch with his teammate in the goal with a back pass

Game situations in which the ball carrier has to play against a numerical majority are considered more difficult than playing 2 vs. 2. Attacking behavior should be developed first before improving defensive skills. The reason for this is that all technical abilities first need to be executed successfully. Thus, following the methodological principle of working from simple to complex, the 1 vs. 2 situation would be implemented after restricting behavior within supporting situations of 1 + 1 vs. 2, yet before playing 2 vs. 2 unrestricted.

Game Situation: 1 vs. 2 Through the Center

Game situation   Diagram of the situation

   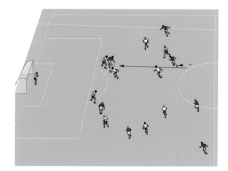

Appropriate exercise taken from the game situation
Level: A simple task to improve 1 vs. 2 ability, Age: 14 years and older

   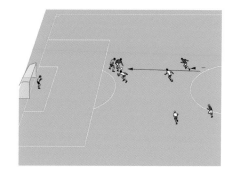

Organization of the exercise (11)
Organization:
- 1 big goal, 1 goalkeeper, 2 defenders vs. 1 attacker in front of the box, 1 attacker behind the goal line as a substitute
- 2 x 4 m counter goals with balls behind them, 10 m behind the midfield line opposite the big goal
- 1 midfielder and 1 defender each in front of the counter goals

Task:

- pass from the midfielder to the attacker followed by supporting run, play to goal
- the defender covers the supporting midfielder
- if the ball is lost, defenders counter the small goals
- after each attack, a new attack by the other midfielders is started
- the attacker can pass the ball back to the midfielder in front of the other counter goal to start a new attack

Topics to be improved:

In Attack	In Defense
Dribbling	Marking/Covering
Support	Double-teaming/Challenging the ball

Modifications to the exercise

in favor of the attack

- the second defender can play only after the attacker has received the ball
- no defending midfielder
- no tackling by the defenders
- the attacking midfielder from the other side can also support

in favor of the defense

- the attacking midfielder must play two-touch
- the forward may not play back to the midfielder, must play 1 vs. 2 to goal (be sure to switch the midfielders and forwards)
- the defending midfielder can challenge the ball carrier as well
- the first ball must be played in the air to the attacker in front

Small-sided game to improve 1 vs. 2 abilities
Organization:
- 2 big goals with keepers 40 m opposite each other a marked midfield line
- 2 teams, distributed as 1 attacker each in front of 1 goal, 2 midfielders behind the midline on the wings and 2 defenders vs. the attacker in each half

Task:
- play 1 vs. 2 to one goal after controlling a pass from one midfielder
- the attacker can play back to a midfielder from his team and switch roles with him
- if the ball is won by defending team, counter pass to one of their midfielders who plays on to the forwards, 1 vs. 2 to the other goal
- after each attempt, attack the same goal following a goalkeeper's throw to one of his midfielders
- playing time: 10 minutes

Variations of the small-sided game
- defenders start from the goal line after the ball has been played to the attacker
- the covering midfielders can close the passing lane to avoid the ball being played to the attacker
- time restriction: finishing within 15 seconds
- midfielders can support and play inside their own half along the entire midfield line

Situations 2 vs. 2

COMBINING 2 vs. 2
- through the center
- on the wing
- in the midfield

5.2.2   Game Situations 2 vs. 2 Through the Center

Game situation   **Diagram of the situation**

Appropriate exercise taken from the game situation
Level: A simple task to improve 2 vs. 2 play without any method-related restrictions, Age: 12 years and older

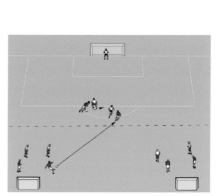

Organization of the exercise (12)
Organization:
- 1 big goal with a goalkeeper; 2 x 5 m goals placed at midfield.
- 12 players, divided in 3 groups of 4 playing 2 vs. 2 each, one group on the big goal, the other two on each of the smaller counter goals

Objective:
- pass from counter goal to one of the attackers for attack 2 vs. 2 on the big goal
- when defenders win the ball, they counterattack by passing the ball to one of their teammates of one group who attack 2 vs. 2 on a small goal

Topics to be improved:

In Attack	In Defense
Supporting	Marking
Creating/using spaceTransition	
Finishing	
Transition	

Modifications to the exercise

in favor of the attack
- the defenders can challenge the ball only after one of the attackers has controlled it
- the attacker who started the exercise with the pass can support the attack from behind
- the attacking ball carrier can pass the ball to a supporting teammate from another goal and switch roles with that player defenders may not tackle

in favor of the defense
- a defensive teammate from another goal can pursue after an attacker has controlled the ball
- require a specific combination to be performed by the attackers
- the first pass to initiate an attack must be played like a drop ball into the air
- a defenders' teammates can defend at the midfield as the ball is brought into play

Small-sided game to improve combination play in 2 vs. 2
Organization:
- 2 goals 25 m opposite each other
- two teams of 6 players each, divided 2 pairs each on the goal line beside the goal and 1 pair playing 2 vs. 2 in the field
- 1 goalkeeper in each goal

Objective:
- play 2 vs. 2
- after finishing, the defending pair comes off the field while the next pair (from the defending team) immediately starts an attack with their own ball. The previously attacking pair remain in the field to defend (transition).
- Playing time: 6 – 8 minutes

Variations of the small-sided game

- predetermined combinations to be executed before scoring
- both teams of two leave the field after a goal and are immediately replaced by two new teams of two
- time rule: a shot must be taken within 10 seconds of the previous shot
- goalkeepers can play in the field

Game Situation: 2 vs. 2 on the Wing

Game situation   Diagram of the situation

Appropriate exercise taken from the game situation
Level: A simple task to improve playing 2 vs. 2 without any method-related restrictions, Age: 12 years and older

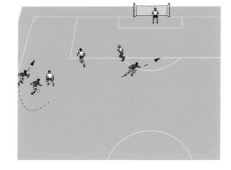

Organization of the exercise (13)
Organization:
- 2 big goals, 35 m opposite each other with 2 goalkeepers
- 2 attackers play against 1 defender on each wing; 1 central attacker against 2 defenders in front of the penalty area
- 1 central player from the defending team plays in front of the attacker's goal

Objective:
- after receiving the ball from the goalkeeper, attack 2 vs. 2 on the wing in an effort to cross the ball to the forward inside the penalty area
- the central player of the defending team can support as well defend in the wings
- after each attempt on the goal, the next attack starts from the attackers' goal
- if the defenders win the ball, they counterattack the opposite goal

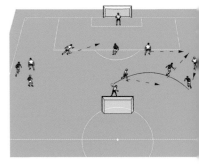

Additional topics to be improved (13):

In Attack	In Defense
Support	Defending
Crossing	Double-teaming
Transition	

Modifications to the exercise
in favor of the attack
- the central player on the defending team may not defend
- change the point of the attack to the other side, if needed
- the central attacker in front of the goal can support the players on the wings
- the attackers on the opposite wing can enter the penalty area to score

in favor of the defense
- the central player of the defending team may defend in front of the goal
- the defender on the opposite wing can move inside to defend in front of the goal
- play using the offside rule
- require a specific combination before shooting

Small-sided game to improve 2 vs. 2 play on the wing
Organization:
- 2 big goals, 32 m opposite each other (double penalty box)
- field divided into 3 parts by the sidelines of the penalty box extended to the goal line of the second goal
- two teams, divided into 1 goalkeeper, 2 vs. 2 each in each wing and 1 central player in the offensive area

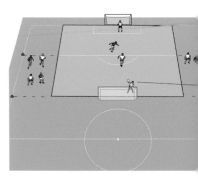

Objective:
- attacking on the wings only, 2 vs. 2
- crossing from the wing, finishing by the central player only
- the goalkeeper can be used to change the point of attack
- the central players can attack only in their half but can defend on the wing
- the wingers can run into their own defending third to defend against the central opponent
- every attack is started by a pass from the goalkeeper to one of the wingers
- playing time: 10 minutes

Variations of the small-sided game
- play 2 vs. 1 on the wings; the defending player in the center can support his teammate in the wing
- goals can be scored only following a winger's ground ball which comes back from the end-line
- smaller game: 1 vs. 1 on each wing, the teammate in the central zone can support his teammate on one wing while the opposite wing player enters the goal area to score
- shots in the central zone must be taken with one-touch only

Game Situation: 2 vs. 2 in the Midfield

Situations of 2 vs. 2 in the midfield can be neglected because there is usually more than just one supporting player near the ball as the attack is being built up. This is because players from both teams move into the midfield area to create a numerical majority on the ball. 1 vs. 1 situations can be avoided due to the multiple options to pass the ball. This should lead to a safe build-up of the play and no lost time which could be taken advantage of by the defending team.

Thus, game situations in the midfield will be trained in the following section using a 3 vs. 3 model.

Situations 3 vs. 3

PLAYING 3 vs. 3
Triangle - "the third man"

- through the center
- building up an attack in the midfield
- countering through the midfield
- on the wing

Playing 3 vs. 3 presents the option to unexpectedly switch the attack to another side and in an entirely new direction. This is due to the mobility of the third man. When two attackers play together, their inter-passing forces the defense to focus on the space and direction in which the attack seems to be going. The defenders concentrate on and shift to cover that side. This opens space on the other side for the sudden involvement of the "third man." Playing 3 vs. 3, then, is mostly based on the options of combining 2 vs. 2. These options deal with two tactical objectives: to change the point of attack in order to avoid a turnover and to beat a delaying opponent in order to quickly gain space and time for an "easier" attempt on goal. The latter idea of 3 players using quick, short passes is often referred to as "triangular play." Thus, the behavior and actions of the third player depends on and should be tactically related to the current situation and the movement of the other players.

5.2.3   Game Situations 3 vs. 3 Through the Center

Game situation   **Diagram of the situation**

   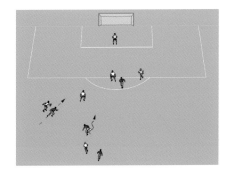

Appropriate exercise taken from the game situation
Level: A simple task to improve playing 3 vs. 3 through the center
          Age: 12 years and older

   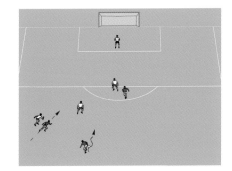

Organization of the exercise (14)
Organization:
- 1 big goal, 1 goalkeeper, two 4 m counter goals, 10 m inside the touch line, 35 m opposite the big goal, marked midline
- 9 players, divided into 3 defenders vs. 3 attackers in the field, 3 more attackers behind the counter goals

Objective:

- Beginning with the dribbling of one of the attackers behind the counter goals into the field, the attacking team plays 3 vs. 3 to the big goal.
- The attacker nearest to the ball carrier moves back behind the counter goals and changes roles with the ball carrier (in the game: covering the attack)
- The offside rule is in effect between the marked midfield line and the goal; every new attack (after a goal or dead ball) has to begin with the dribbling of another attacker behind the counter goals.
- If a defender wins the ball, he counterattacks on the small goals. Switch defensive and offensive teams.

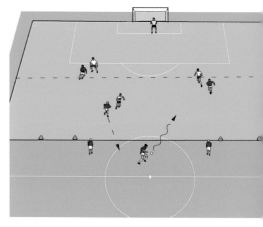

Additional topics to be improved (14):

In Attack	In Defense
Support	Marking and taking over
Creating space	Use of offside rule
Mobility	

Modifications to the exercise

in favor of the attackers

- no offside rule
- defenders may only challenge after the attackers first touch
- no role change after the first pass, but rather the attacker supports from behind, making it 4 vs. 3
- the attacking team can pass back to one of the waiting attackers at any time, which results in the passing and receiving players switching roles

in favor of the defenders

- no switching of roles in the attacking team
- ball must be kept on the ground
- the goalkeeper may leave the goal to play with the defending three
- a defender can be placed behind the counter goals who recovers once the first pass by the attacking team has been received

Small-sided game to improve 3 vs. 3 finishing

Organization:
- Marked field 20 x 30 m with two goals, a middle line, 2 neutral goalkeepers
- 2 teams of 5 players each divided into 2 vs. 2 in one half, 1 vs. 1 in the other half, 1 winger each outside of the touchline

Objective:

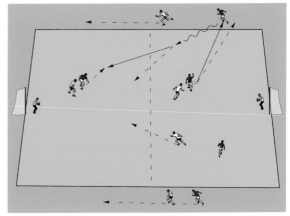

- Build up an attack of 2 vs. 2 in one half, progress by passing to the target player in the other half who finishes on goal
- A pass to one of the wingers results in the winger entering the field and the passer coming off to wait in the wing
- The wing players support in their corresponding halves
- An attack can be started only after having made at least one change with a winger and has to be finished without using a winger
- After having played the ball into the attacking half, one defender can enter the area to defend with his teammate
- The player who plays the target player in the other half may enter into that half, making it 2 vs. 2
- Possession remains with the team who shoots (regardless of whether the goal is scored)
- Playing time: 8 – 10 minutes

Variations of the small-sided game:
- no goalkeepers, the marking defender plays as both a defender and goalkeeper
- the wide players play 1 vs. 1 outside the touchline
- once a supporting attacker has run over to the midfield to help the target player, he may only be used once; otherwise, possession is given back to the defending team
- one of the two midfielders can enter the attacking half to support

Game Situation: 3 vs. 3
Build-up of an Attack in the Midfield

Game situation   Diagram of the situation

Appropriate exercise taken from the game situation
Level: A simple 3 vs. 3 task to improve the build-up of an attack in midfield
          Age: 12 years and older

Organization of the exercise (15)
Organization:
- 1 big goal with keeper; two 3 m counter goals, 40 m opposite the big goal, 10 m inside each touchline
- 1 attacker vs. 1 defender inside the box
- 3 attackers vs. 3 defenders in the midfield; 3 substitute attackers behind the counter goals

Objective:
- 3 vs. 3 in midfield; a goal can be scored only after having passed the ball to the attacker in the box
- the attacker in the box can play inside the box only
- if defender wins the ball, he counterattacks on the small goals
- change the attacking team after each goal (remember to change the defenders with the attackers as well)

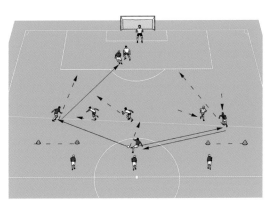

Additional topics to be imroved (15):

In Attack	In Defense
Passing	Delaying
Support	Shifting
Dribbling	Communication

Modifications to the exercise
in favor of the attackers
- attacker in the box plays unmarked, two-touch only
- the ball can be passed back to one of the players behind the counter goals to maintain possession
- a pass back to the one of the players behind the goal results in a role change between the two
- teams can score from outside the box as well

in favor of the defenders
- passes must be kept on the ground
- finish within 30 seconds
- the defender in the box can leave the box to defend as well
- the defenders in the midfield can enter the box to support the single defender

Small-sided game to improve the build-up of an attack in the midfield
Organization:
- marked field 20 x 30 m, marked midfield line, 2 goals
- two teams of 6 players each, divided into 1 goalkeeper, 2 substitutes in the corners of the opponents field, 3 players each in the field

Objective:
- maintain ball possession 3 vs. 3 in the field
- passing to a substitute = changing roles with him
- goals count only after having passed the ball across the midfield to a substitute and executing a change of roles
- five consecutive passes in one half of the field also equals one goal
- playing time: 6 to 8 minutes

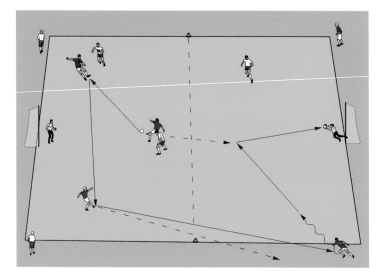

Variations of the small-sided game
- no goals, goalkeepers or scoring, just maintain ball possession
- each pass to a substitute in the other half equals one goal
- passing allowed on the ground only
- substitutes can move along the goal and touchlines of the half in which they're playing
- no goals, substitutes from the same team play diagonally to one another

Game Situation: 3 vs. 3
Counterattack Through the Midfield

Game situation

Diagram of the situation

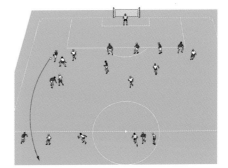

Appropriate exercise taken from the game situation
Level: A simple 3 vs. 3 task to improve the build-up of an attack in midfield
        Age: 14 years and older

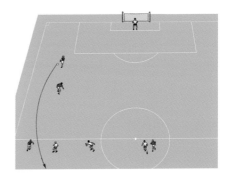

Organization of the exercise (16)
Organization:
- 2 big goals, 40 m opposite each other with 1 goalkeeper each
- 4 groups of 3 players each, placed as 3 defenders and 3 attackers between the goals, two groups waiting behind one goal with extra balls in that goal

Objective:

- The three defenders play 3 vs. 1 against one of the red attackers. The other attackers wait next to the goal.
- as soon as the ball is shot on goal the goalkeeper immediately plays against one of the three attackers, who counter on the opposite goal
- After a goal, the three defenders who were just scored on attack 3 vs. 1 against the next counter group while the last group moves back into waiting position

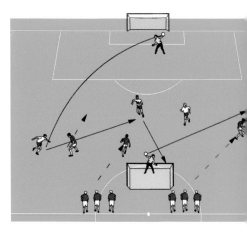

Additional topics to be imroved (16):

In Attack	In Defense
Supporting	Delaying
Finishing	

Modifications to the exercise

in favor of the attackers

- 11 meter semicircle in front of the counter goal. The defenders have to finish from inside this circle
- attacking players (to be improved) defend with two players instead of one (3 vs. 2)
- defending team changes roles only after they've scored
- no tackling

in favor of the defenders

- marked midfield line, offside rule is in effect in attacking half
- passes must be on the ground
- time rule; attacking team has 15 seconds to finish once ball is played from goalkeeper
- one additional defender recovers from behind the counter goal once the goalkeeper's pass has been received

Small-sided game to improve 3 vs. 3 countering through the midfield
Organization:
- marked field 20 x 30 m with 2 goals, 2 neutral goalkeepers, marked midfield line
- 3 teams of 3 players each

Objective:
- play 3 vs. 3 within one half of the field; the 3rd team waits on the goal line of the opposite goal
- after a goal or loss of possession, immediately counter on the opposite goal
- after having lost the ball, the attacking team can defend up to the midfield line
- as soon as the ball passes the midfield line, the waiting team can enter the field to defend against the countering team.
- the previous attackers wait on the opposite goal line
- playing time: 8 to 10 minutes

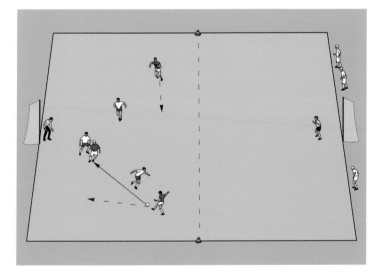

Variations of the small-sided game
- no goalkeepers, one of the three defenders has to play in the goal as well as defense (3 vs. 2+1)
- time rule: score within eight seconds after having won the ball
- team that scores keeps possession and goes the other way, while the defending team can defend up to the midfield line
- one neutral player on each touchline, always playing with the attacking team

Game Situation:
3 vs. 3 on the Wing

Game situation   Diagram of the situation

   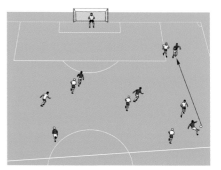

Appropriate exercise taken from the game situation
Level: A simple task to improve 3 vs. 3 play on the wing
          Age: 14 years and older

   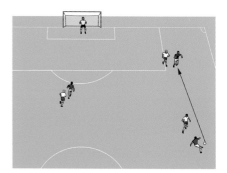

Organization of the exercise (17)
Organization:
- 1 big goal with keeper; 2 counter lines, 10 m each, 35 m opposite the big goal, 5 m inside the touchlines
- 2 attackers against 2 defenders on each wing, 1 central attacker against a central defender in the box, 1 central midfielder against a defensive midfielder between the counter lines; 20 balls in the midfield circle

Objective:
- alternate attacks on each wing, the objective is to cross to the central attacker who finishes
- the central attacker can also support the wing attack prior to the cross
- following a goal, a new attack with the next ball by the central midfielder on the other wing is started
- the central midfielder can support the attack from behind
- when defenders win the ball, they counterattack to the line-goals
- the defensive midfielder can support the counterattack to the line-goals
- a goal is scored when the ball is played over the line the defensive midfielder

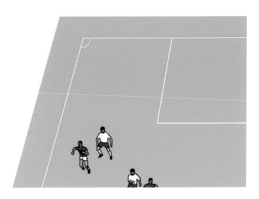

Additional topics to be imroved (17):

In Attack	In Defense
Dribbling	Marking/Covering
Supporting	Crossing

Modifications to the exercise

in favor of the attackers
- no defender in the box, the central attacker has to finish, two-touch
- the opponent of the central attacker can defend inside the box only
- the attacking team can change the point of attack from one wing to the other one if needed
- the attackers from the opposite wing enter the box to support and finish

in favor of the defenders
- attack on the wing only successful after having performed a specific combination
- the wing and central defenders can shift to the ball side to assist the other two defenders
- the central attacker must play one-touch
- the central attacker must play two-touch

Small-sided game to improve 3 vs. 3 play on the wing

Organization:

- field of 45 x 30 m, marked into 3 thirds of 15 x 30 m each, 2 big goals with goalkeepers on the middle third;
- 2 teams of 6 players each, distributed 2 vs. 2 in the wing thirds and 1 vs. 1 in the middle third in front of each goal Objective:
- Play 6 vs. 6, however, all players have to play within their third of the field
- Each attack must be played over a ing and finished after a cross with one touch of each player being involved; the central players must play two-touch
- playing time: 10 minutes

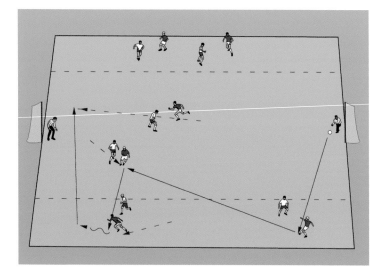

Variations of the small-sided game

- the team which scores keeps possession and goes the other way
- don't play 2 vs. 2 in the middle zone, but rather let the players from the opposite wing move into the middle zone to finish (4 vs. 4)
- additional option: change the point of attack to the opposite wing
- play without goalkeepers: the defending player in the middle zone plays both as defender and goalkeeper.

Situations with Numerical Advantage

- in the defending zone 4 vs. 2
- in the midfield zone 4 vs. 3

Each of the exercises described above can be modified into a task of numerical advantage for either the players in attack or in defense. This is a way to increase or decrease the topic's requirement within the exercise. These modifications are sometimes necessary to adjust the requirements of an exercise to the players' level of performance.

The following section deals with game situations of attack in which a numerical advantage usually occurs due to the teams' systems and their tactical strategies or defensive break down. Experts generally agree that to learn and improve attacking is much more difficult than defending and, thus, attacking should be practiced first. How to defend successfully should be improved as a means of increasing the requirements of the practiced situation. Therefore, this section focuses on how to make use of the numerical advantage when building up an attack from the defense deep in the midfield. This is because defenders usually move forward into the midfield to support their teammates in order to reach the shooting area as fast but as securely as possible.

Two typical situations of a numerical advantage of 4 vs. 2 (defense) and 4 vs. 3 (midfield) are taken as an example for practice. Both samples can easily be modified into similar situations including less or more players. Those modifications are useful when, for example, the training is focused in particular on the midfield play within the systems of 4-4-2 and 3-5-2.

5.2.4 Game Situations: 4 vs. 2 in the Defending Zone

Game situation	**Diagram of the situation**

Appropriate exercise taken from the game situation

Level: A simple task to improve 4 vs. 2 play in the defending zone
        Age: 12 years and older

	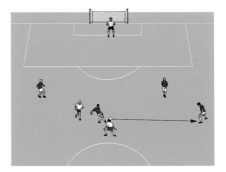

Organization of the exercise (18)
Organization:
- marked field 40 x 60 m, 2 big goals with goalkeepers, several balls in each goal
- 4 players defend their goal vs. 2 strikers, 1 vs. 1 in front of the opposite goal

Objective:
- 4 defenders build up an attack and try to score vs. 2 opponents after receiving the ball from their goalkeeper
- the defenders must use their striker first before crossing the midfield to support him
- if the ball is won by the other team (2 forwards), they try to score on the opposite goal
- the goalkeeper restarts each play with a pass to one of the 4 defenders in front of his goal.

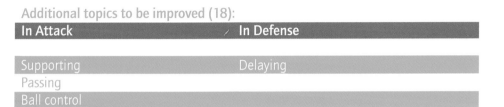

Additional topics to be improved (18):

In Attack	In Defense
Supporting	Delaying
Passing	
Ball control	

Modifications to the exercise
in favor of the 4 defending players
- play 1 vs. 2 or 2 vs. 2 instead of 1 vs. 1 in front of the opposite goal
- the strikers can only delay or chase the ball within their attacking zone
- make the field wider (between the two touch lines)
- the goalkeeper can start an attack with a long pass to the target forward

in favor of the 2 strikers
- 4 vs. 3 in back rather than 4 vs. 2
- exercise starts with a long ball played from the opposing goalkeeper to his two forwards
- passes must be on the ground only
- play 3 defenders vs. 2 strikers

Small-sided game to improve playing with a numerical advantage

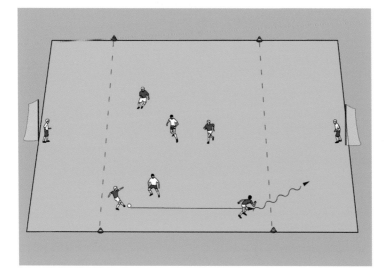

Organization:
- 2 goals, 40 m opposite each other
- marked field 20 x 30 m
- 2 teams of 4 players each

Objective:
- play 4 vs. 2 from one end line over the opposite end line
- the ball carrier must dribble over the line, after which he can go to the goal
- following a goal, attack the opposite line and goal
- if the defenders or goalkeeper win the ball, both teams change roles
- playing time: 8 minutes

Variations of the small-sided game

- the players in the goals can defend at the line
- the ball must be passed over the line to a teammate before going to the goal
- all passes must be on the ground
- time rule: the team in possession has 15 seconds to cross the line and go to the goal

5.2.5 Game Situation: 4 vs. 3 in the Midfield

Game situation

Diagram of the situation

Appropriate exercise taken from the game situation

Level: A simple task to improve 4 vs. 3 play in the midfield
        Age: 13 years and older

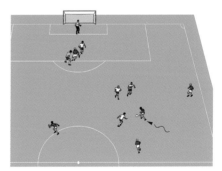

Organization of the exercise (19)
Organization:

- 1 big goal with goalkeeper, 2 small goals 3 m each, 10 m inside the touchline at the midfield line
- marked line 20 m from the end line dividing the half-field into a midfield and an attacking zone
- 4 vs. 3 attacking in the midfield zone, 1 vs. 2 in the attacking zone

Objective:
- 4 vs. 3 build up of an attack followed by finding the target forward who goes to the goal
- the striker can only play in the attacking zone, the defenders can support their teammates and defend in the midfield zone
- the attacking midfielders can move into the attacking zone only after having passed the ball to the striker first
- after the attack is finished, the goalkeeper plays the ball back to the midfield line for the next attack
- if the defenders win the ball, they counter on the small goals

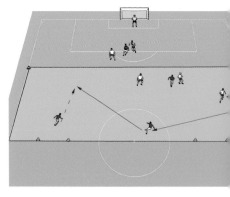

Additional topics to be improved (19):

In Attack	In Defense
Supporting	Delaying
Dribbling	

Modifications to the exercise

in favor of the attackers
- the ball carrier in midfield can dribble into the attacking zone and shoot
- two additional small goals, 2 m wide, on each touchline 25 m from the end line to also be played to by the attacking midfielders
- defenders in the defensive zone may not enter the midfield zone to assist
- two strikers in the attacking zone vs. the two defenders

in favor of the defenders
- ball must be played from the midfield to the striker within a given amount of time
- restrict the number of ball touches in the midfield zone
- the defenders of the midfield zone can also defend in the defending zone
- attacking team must keep all passes on the ground

Small-sided game to improve the build-up of an attack with a numerical advantage

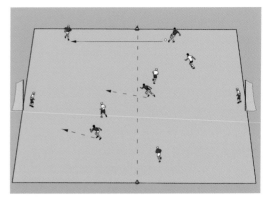

Organization:
- field of 20 x 30 m, marked midline, 2 large goals
- 2 teams of 5 players each

Objective:
- 5 vs. 5 on both goals
- the defending team has to put one player as a goalkeeper in each goal, so that in the field the game becomes 5 vs. 3
- the attacking team can finish on both goals after a goal is scored, possession remains with the team that scored.
- after every goal or change of possession, the ball has to be played over the midline at least once before another goal can be scored
- when the defending team wins the ball, the two goalkeepers go into the field to attack, while the other team has to put two players into the goal before being able to challenge the ball
- playing time: 6 to 10 minutes

Variations of the small-sided game
- the goalkeeper can defend everywhere in his half (5 vs. 4)
- the ball must be played on ground
- the ball has to be played with two touches
- play with neutral goalkeepers, 5 vs. 5 on both goals

6 THE GOALKEEPER DETERMINES THE TEAM'S SUCCESS

6.1 General Aspects

Rules and Requirements

There are special rules concerning the goalkeeper's play in soccer. These rules relate to his behavior within the penalty box. Within this area the goalkeeper can use his hands to catch and play the ball. Additionally, within the six-yard box the goalkeeper is not allowed to be challenged by opponents.

"Many Goalkeepers destroy their good positioning by too much movement!"

These rules lead to special technical and tactical skills which are required to perform the basic task of saving the ball. However, additional rules require the keeper to improve all the basic abilities of a field player as well. These rules are (i) the keeper is not allowed to use his hands inside the box when the ball is intentionally played to him from the foot of a teammate (in contrast to another part of the body) and (ii) when outside of the box he has to follow the rules of field players. This means the goalkeeper should improve the skills to control and play the ball with his feet as well as his tactical understanding of the game. He must foresee the development of the current situation, then coach and guide his teammates as a result of his free, unchallenged position on the field.

Additionally, the keeper should improve general physical abilities, aerobic endurance to hold concentration over the entire game, muscular strength for jumping, diving and running to save the ball and power to perform these actions quickly and dynamically. In order to play the game successfully, the goalkeeper needs a high degree of coordination (agility and flexibility).

Considering that the goalkeeper plays mostly inside the penalty area, which means less motion in general, the training of this position must be special and extend well beyond his practicing with and as a field player.

During the years of learning and improving technical skill as a goalkeeper, there is another aspect which must be considered, especially for training young goalkeepers. Children should learn to catch, punch and save the ball in practice, without gloves. It is important to improve the feeling and hold on the ball with the fingers as soon as possible. This perspective can be seen when observing the improvement of soccer skills in the poor countries of Africa and South America. Many children still play soccer without shoes, just barefoot. Later on, when observing their technical development, most of them display an outstanding ability to handle the ball with their feet, despite the lack of systematic training early in their childhood.

Specialization and Biological Preconditions

There are some good reasons why a goalkeeper should not begin his career before the age of 11 or 12. Up to that age every child is pretty much able to play successfully in the goal. Nearly all children like to play and move like a keeper in the goal during both training and games. It is also difficult to select the one who shows the promise of becoming a successful goalkeeper later in life. Experience has told us that a child's decision to become a goalkeeper develops much later, with little or no influence from the outside and doesn't even always have to do with their height.

Another rationale for a goalkeeper's training as a field player is based on the early development of general coordination. Children often begin to play soccer in teams which are under 10 years of age. This is an advantage for the development and improvement of basic coordination and aerobic as well as anaerobic endurance. In soccer, field players must run, jump, kick and move around on the field. A goalkeeper, however, mostly observes the others playing. His responsibilities and position force him to stand and to wait for the ball.

When entering a duel with the ball carrier, the goalkeeper must be ready to come out to either side and react when the player gives him a chance to get the ball. If the ball carrier tries to pass him by dribbling or shoots, he must be able to jump and dive, catch or deflect and play the ball out of the attacker's control. This requires a high level of courage and risk-taking.

Separate goalkeeper training requires an appropriate level of physical condition regarding agility and flexibility. This is needed in order to execute and improve different goalkeeper-specific movements successfully. Agility and flexibility depend

on the development of the muscles of the arms, legs and rest of the body, especially the abdomen. These muscles are still developing up to the age of 8 or 9.

Therefore, the following general principles of goalkeeper training should be adhered to:
- All children up through the start of puberty, in particular at the beginning of their soccer career, should learn the basic movements and skills for improving agility and flexibility.
- The goalkeeper should practice and improve his skills as a field player as well.
- The decision to become a goalkeeper should be up to the player.
- Special goalkeeper training should begin after the player's decision to become a keeper, but not before the age of 9 or 10. However, exercises to catch, hold and save a ball easily should be trained in fun games from the beginning. This is to improve coordinative abilities which the goalkeeper will require later on.
- The goalkeeper should play as a field player in games to improve endurance and game experience.

Training and the Requirements in the Game
A fundamental aspect of training focuses on developing skills and behaviors which are needed during competition. The goalkeeper needs aerobic endurance in order to concentrate throughout the entire game. In contrast to a field player, he does not need endurance in strength and speed, however, he does need sheer strength and power. A dive takes but a couple of seconds, although sometimes the goalkeeper has to perform multiple actions one after the other. However, after having been active the keeper generally has enough time to fully recover before the next required action. This is in contrast to field players. The minutes spent observing guarantee that his body will replenish the energy lost by the previous action.

With these differences in mind, goalkeeper training should replicate similar game conditions, i.e. time enough to recover between intense but short bouts. A goalkeeper does not have to jump and run during a game without a break like field players. This would then require the physical ability of strength endurance. For the goalkeeper it is important to jump as high as he can, to dive as quick as he can or to run out of his goal as fast as he can, just once. These actions require explosiveness, this is the maximum combination of power and speed. The training principles for muscular endurance demand a series of actions with short breaks not long enough for full recovery. Explosiveness itself, however, requires the highest intensity but for a goalkeeper this means just once or twice followed by a break, in which he can recover completely. To improve this physical ability the so-called repetition method has to be used. This means actions executed with the highest intensity but with plenty of time in between so that the next action can be

The rules allow the goalkeeper to take his time after having won the ball in order to allow his team to leave the box and to organize before he distributes the ball again. This is nearly enough time for a complete recovery.

performed after having completely recovered. As a training implication, then, the goalkeeper should never get out of breath during training.

To practice what is required in the game also relates to the way exercises themselves are designed. There will never be a game situation in which several players shoot on goal one after the other without stopping. Exercises should be constructed as combined tasks the way they occur in the game. To practice under game-related, situational conditions first requires the improvement of special skills and abilities. Some exercises can be practiced without additional field players, others should be trained with field players, in particular those which relate to tactical behavior.

Even the goalkeeper should improve all required abilities in game-like situations. Technical skills and their appropriate usage should still be practiced during the so-called "golden years" (best learning years). Later on, exercises will be developed into more complex situations in order to work on tactical skills and behavior.

Based on these aspects, the following chapters describe the required skills and explain how they are successfully used in a match via relevant exercise examples. Regarding the basic aspects mentioned above, however, other similar exercises could also be constructed.

A goalkeeper's training is often more or less individual. This is because the position and tasks of the goalkeeper are quite different to those of the field players and thus need special exercises to improve both technical and tactical abilities. Many individual exercises are described in textbooks and practiced in training sessions all over the world, however the goalkeeper must first be considered a member of the team. Goalkeeper training should be linked to all of the attacking and defending situations of a game. The offensive and defensive behaviors of a goalkeeper are nearly always influenced by other players. Decisions to be made when catching or punching a high ball in front of the goal, for example, depends on the situation. Similarly, the situation can also dictate decisions like whether to distribute on the ground to an outside back or punt the ball across midfield to the forwards. Therefore, in addition to individual drills, exercises which improve technical and tactical abilities in typical defending situations which are related and include all the necessary field players are also very important.

There are some remarkable advantages to be gained by involving field players in a goalkeeper's training session.

1　The coach is free to observe and to correct mistakes.

2　The field players can train specific techniques or movements as well.

3　Due to the concept of transition, the goalkeeper learns that saving the ball and keeping possession is much better than simply saving it regardless of whether or not it goes out of bounds.

4　The intention to build-up the attack immediately after gaining possession of the ball influences decisions of how to defend and therefore increases continuous attention to the ongoing game.

5　Stoppages in order to make corrections allow time for the goalkeeper to recover before the next repetition. This, as already mentioned above, is necessary so that the goalkeeper has full concentration and can exert maximum power with each save.

Based on this, only one exercise is provided for each technical or tactical topic to be improved. These samples demonstrate how game situations can be constructed for specialized goalkeeper training. Additionally, these examples should be modified by coaches according to the goalkeepers level and reconstructed into other game-related exercises for goalkeeper training.

6.2   Basic Skills

Basic goalkeeping skills are those technical abilities which are mostly used throughout the game due to the keeper's position and the fact that he can play the ball with his hands.

Catching balls as well as diving and saving shots are skills which all children like to do during their free time. These are also skills they learn in school physical education programs. With this in mind, such skills can also be considered appropriate for improving basic coordination. They should therefore be practiced by all children right from the start and even later on by field players in order to stabilize and improve agility and flexibility. A player needs to be able to balance his body using his hands when jumping, falling and even kicking with the right and left leg (weight on one leg). Thus, simple exercises to catch or dive to save a ball should be utilized as fundamental tasks for all children before starting specialized goalkeeper training.

The goal kick and punting of the ball need to be mentioned as well. However, kicking and passing are clearly related to the techniques of all soccer players and therefore described in previous chapters. In contrast, punting is a special skill of using the hands (throwing) for distribution. It should get a special focus within the goalkeeper's skills.

Catching the Ball in the Air
Coaching points
- fingers spread out
- both thumbs pointing inwards towards each other behind the ball
- pressure on the ball (from the hands) below its midline
- catch with arms extended
- catch the ball over the head
- bring the ball down at once to secure it against the body

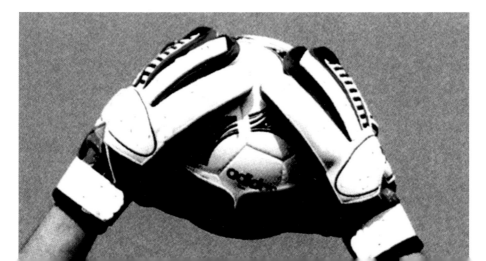

Activity example
Organization:
- two goals, 30 m opposite each other
- 1 keeper in each goal
- 8 players divided into 4 pairs with 1 ball each

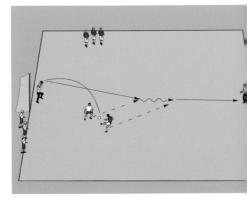

Objective:
- 1 player, 16 m in front of the trained keeper's goal and 3 m in front of his partner (defender), volleys the ball from his hands over his opponent.
- when the goalkeeper catches the ball, he throws it to the running defender, who finishes on the opposite goal against the attacker (who's now a defender)
- if the goalkeeper can't keep the ball (rebound), the field players are free to go 1 vs. 1.
- players switch with those waiting

Catching the Ball Between the Waist and Chest
Coaching points
- hands together, palms up, close to the body
- fingers spread out to keep hands around the ball
- entire body behind the ball
- elbows close to the body
- catch the ball as if it were entering a funnel
- stable stance or land on both feet if having jumped
- exert inward pressure on the ball with the fingers

Activity example
Organization:
- 1 goal 5 x 2 m, keepers take turns
- 2 small 3 m goals, each 25 m opposite the keepers' goal in line with the extended penalty area
- 8 players, divided into two groups, two beside the goal, each with a ball, and two across between the small goals

Objective:
- the player on the goal line passes the ball on the ground towards his teammate, who's outside the box, and the teammate finishes with one or two touches
- if the keeper catches the shot, he makes a transitional throw into one of the small goals = 1 goal for the keeper
- the shooting player can try to defend the goals against the throw
- the competition is between the two groups and the keeper
- players change roles after six shots each

Saving Medium-height and High Shots
Coaching Points
- quick short step or two if time to push off and dive with the ball-side foot
- reach toward the ball with the closer hand
- closer hand guides the body
- dive straight to the ball (direct, shortest route) and deflect the ball away from the goal
- stabilize hand (firm) before contact
- "push" the ball sideways if unable to catch it with both hands

Activity example
Organization:
- 1 big goal with keeper in a marked penalty box
- 2 small goals, 2 m, on the corners of the box
- 2 groups of 4 players each divided into pairs, 1 vs. 1 inside the box on each side; 2 pairs at the top of the box

Objective:
- Taking turns, one player outside the box shoots the ball using two-touch.
- Alternate between teams.
- If the goalkeeper saves and holds the ball, he transitions by throwing to the opposite team in the box, who attack the small goals. The exercise then starts again from outside the box.

- If the goalkeeper saves the ball but doesn't hold it, the ball is free for one of the players inside the box to finish. Switch roles. After a goal, the same player from outside the box starts again.

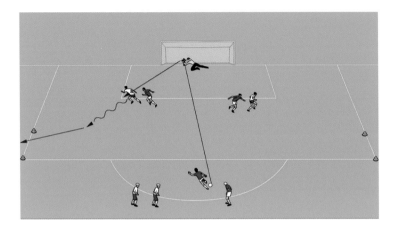

6.3   Special Skills

Special skills of the goalkeeper relate to difficult game situations in which a basic skill has to be used in a particular manner in order to solve the problem presented. These technical skills to save and/or hold the ball are based on the goalkeeper's ability to perform the basic skill first. For this reason, special skills should be improved only once the goalkeeper has gained experience using the basic techniques in the game.

Saving Low Shots at the Body
Coaching points

- catch a ball being shot directly at you or slightly off to one side as described above
- use quick sideways steps, if time allots, to get the body behind the ball
- bring the arms and hands up to meet the ball (away from the goal)
- open the hands and keep the elbows close together
- lean forward towards the ball and go down on the knees
- secure the ball in front of the body

Activity example

Organization:
- 1 small goal (2 x 5) with the keeper being trained, 1 big goal 40 m opposite, shooting line marked 16 m in front of the small goal
- two teams of 4 players each

Objective:
- player of the defending team shoots a low ball at the small goal
- if the keeper catches the ball, he throws to a member of the opposite team to play 4 vs. 4 on both goals (30 sec. limit)
- after finishing or time limit, the next shot is taken by the team which scored last
- if the shot misses the goal, one point is awarded to the other team however a new shot is taken by the same team
- if the goalkeeper cannot hold the ball (rebound), play 4 vs. 4

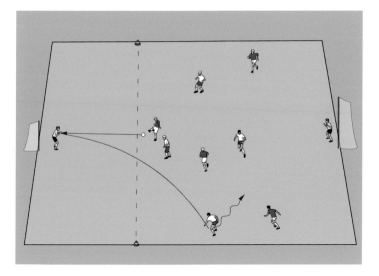

Saving Low Shots at the Feet
Coaching points
- balance the body on the far leg
- kick the ball side leg out from under the body
- get the ball-side hand down quickly to stop the shot (the hand guides the body to the ball)
- stabilize hand (firm) before contact other hand follows to keep the ball on the ground
- immediately secure possession by bringing the ball against the body

Activity example
Organization:
- 2 goals with keepers, 30 m opposite each other
- 1 small, low goal, 3 m wide and half a meter high (gate goal) in the middle of the field, with a keeper
- 2 marked shooting lines, 10 m each from the middle goal
- 2 groups of 4 players each divided into 2 vs. 2 in front of the big goals

Objective:
- Taking turns, one player shoots on the ground from the shooting line at the middle goal.
- If the keeper saves the ball, he throws to a player of the other team in the half where the ball came from. From there, it's 2 vs. 2 at the big goal.
- If the ball crosses the line of the middle goal, 1 goal is scored and the ball is free for one of the opposite players to take and play 2 vs. 2 at the other big goal.
- If the keeper saves the shot but cannot hold it, it's free for the players to take and finish.
- If the defending team wins the ball, they counter to the middle goal.
- After each goal, the activity begins again with a shot from a member of the scoring team on the opposite side.

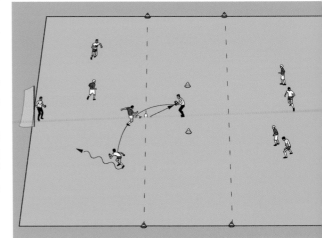

Deflecting Shots on the Ground

Coaching points

- ball-side hand guides the diving body
- stabilize ball-side hand (firm) before contact
- quick side step before diving to jump with the ball-side foot
- dive to the ball, body in a straight line between jumping leg and saving hand
- eyes focused on the ball
- opposite hand follows to secure the ball on the ground

Activity example

Organization:

- 1 goal with keeper
- 2 smaller counter goals, 30 m opposite the big goal, 20 m apart from one another
- 8 players, divided into 3 attacking pairs and 1 defending pair, all at the line of the counter goals

Objective:

- After receiving the ball from the goalkeeper, two attacking players play to goal against one of the defenders; shots must be low the pairs switch after each goal scored if the defender or the goalkeeper win the ball, they counterattack on both small goals
- offensive and defensive pairs change roles (i) after a successful counter, or (ii) when the shot is not on the ground

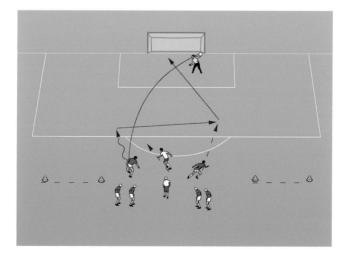

Saving Shots on the Ground on an Imaginary Goal Line
Coaching points
- see also: deflecting shots on the ground
- move towards the ball to narrow the goal line.
- dive into the shot on the imaginary new goal line
- see the ball while diving
- stabilize the hand to stop or push away the ball (parry)
- make a quick decision to save the ball with the second hand (catch)

Activity example
Organization:
- 2 big goals with 1 keeper each, 30 m opposite one another
- 2 cone markers on each side, 10 m out and away from each goal
- 2 groups of 4 players each, 3 vs. 3 between the goals, 1 each outside and behind the cones with a ball

Task:
- first touch towards the endline, second touch shot on goal
- if a goal is scored, another player from the same team shoots in the same manner
- if the goalkeeper catches the ball, he transitions with a throw to his field players who play 3 vs. 3 to the other goal if the ball is lost, the team now in possession counters
- if the goalkeeper saves but doesn't hold the ball (rebound), then play 3 vs. 3 until a goal is scored play to a different goal with each restart of the activity

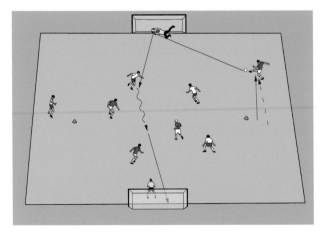

Deflecting High Balls to the Corner
Coaching points
- movement as described above, additionally:
- if the ball is shot above shoulder-height, turn the shoulders toward the ball and use the non ball-side hand
- thus, after having initially guided the body with the ball-side hand, push the ball wide or over the bar
- watch the ball at all times

Activity example
Organization:
- 2 goals with keepers, 25 m opposite each other
- 2 groups of 4 players, the defending players shoulder to shoulder at the penalty spot
- 2 attackers at the top of the box, 1 attacker on each side of the box

Objective:
- 4 defenders act as a wall and try to catch the high shots of the attackers with their hands
- taking turns, the attackers at the top of the box each play the ball over the defenders to score with a high shot; if the keeper saves the ball, he transits by throwing the ball to the defenders, who counter 4 vs. 2 on the opposite goal
- if a goal is scored or the shot missed, the activity starts again with the attackers' shot; after three missed shots in a row, the teams change roles
- if the keeper saves the shot but does not hold it (rebound), the attackers take it and try to pass it back to the shooting attackers; the defenders can try to win the ball and counter
- if a defender catches the ball, the defenders counter 4 vs. 2 on the opposite goal
- if the counter is successful, the teams change roles

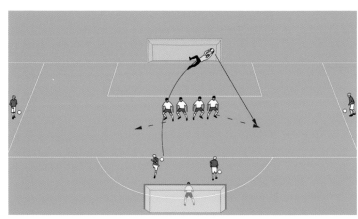

Deflecting Balls Close to the Crossbar
Coaching points
- movements of jumping and diving as described above, additionally:
- run forward to the goal line before jumping to save a high ball with one hand
- watch the ball at all times
- jump to the ball when it's close to the crossbar
- face the bar when pushing the ball over it

Activity example
Organization:
- 2 goals opposite each other at 25 m, 2 keepers
- 1 goal turned around at the top of the box, the other at the midfield circle
- two groups of 4 players, divided into 3 vs. 3 between the goals and 1 server each inside the box in the corners

Objective:
- taking turns, the servers play a ball at the crossbar
- a goalkeeper's save over the bar puts the ball in play on the other side; the team that wins the saved ball attacks 3 vs. 3 on the other goal
- after each goal, the activity starts again with a cross by the other server
- if the defending team or the goalkeeper win the ball, they counter to their own server for another cross
- if the goalkeeper being trained can catch the ball, the next cross comes from the opposite server

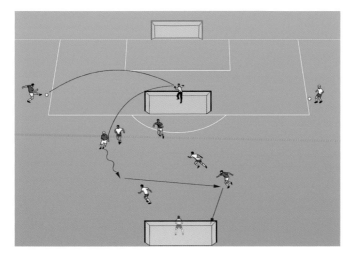

Punching/Boxing
Coaching points

- make a fist with the hand
- hit the ball with the proximal (closest to hand) digits of the fingers
- punch the ball high and out of the box
- punch the ball in the direction it's heading
- punch with the ball-side hand
- punch with one hand when intensely challenged
- use both hands together when punching the ball straight back where it came from

Activity example
Organization:
- 1 goal with the keeper to be trained, 2 small goals opposite the big goal, 2 m each, 30 m apart from one another, a 2nd goalkeeper between them
- 2 teams of 4 players, divided into 2 vs. 2 outside the box, 2 vs. 1 in the box and 1 each on the edges of the penalty area with some balls

Objective:
- taking turns, throw in from the edge of box to the teammate in front of the goal, who tries to finish
- the goalkeeper defends by punching the ball back into the field, after which a 2 vs. 1 situation results toward the small goals vs. the other goalkeeper
- if the defending team wins the ball, they counter on the big goal
- after each goal, the activity starts again with a throw-in

Throwing the Ball
Coaching points
- keep the ball and observe the runs of the players first
- hold the ball securely in one hand
- rotate the shoulder of the ball arm back preparing to increase the power of the throw
- throw with the arm extended
- take a long step forward when throwing
- weight is on one leg as throwing motion is executed
- keep hands and fingers contracted to avoid the ball slipping over the fingers out of the hand
- for shorter distances, use the hand to roll the ball

Activity example
Organization:
- 2 goals with keepers 40 m opposite each other
- 2 teams of 4 players
- 1 neutral player

Objective:
- 4 vs. 4 on both goals
- after each score, the keeper throws to one of his teammates each attack has to be finished within 15 sec.
- the neutral player plays with the team in possession of the ball

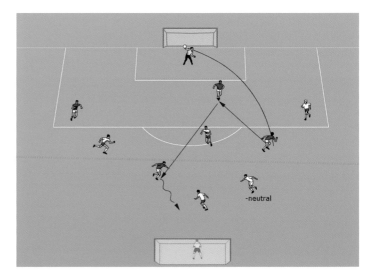

6.4 Basic Tactical Movements

Tactical movements are special goalkeeper behaviors needed to use the technical skills for defending the goal or winning the ball. The distinction between the basic moves of a keeper and his tactical behavior (see Volume II) is made because in order to apply the chosen technical skill, the goalkeeper must first get into the best position to execute this skill. Regarding the didactical philosophy of using game-related exercises, technical abilities should be improved in combination with correct movement. This can already be trained within the first years of systematic training.

The goalkeeper must find the most advantageous position from the middle of the goal line according to the position and distance of the ball in the field.

Regarding the didactical philosophy of using game-related exercises, technical abilities should be improved in combination with correct movement. This can already be taught within the first years of systematic training.

Narrowing the Goal Line
Coaching points
- pay attention to orientation with the middle of the goal line and the ball when moving out of the goal
- move out slowly when the opponent is in possession of the ball, always be ready to react sideways
- delay the opponent's dribble with fewer steps forward
- wait for the opponent to make a move first
- come out only a short distance to avoid the ball being chipped over into the goal

Activity example
Organization:
- marked penalty box with 1 goal and a keeper
- 1 small goal (5 x 2 m) with a keeper, 25 m opposite the big goal
- two groups of 4 players, divided into 4 attackers inside the lines of the box, 2 defenders in the box and 2 outside the box in front of the other goal

Objective:
- play 4 vs. 2 inside the box
- attempt to finish with a sudden shot; if a goal is scored, then the 4 successful players maintain possession
- if the defenders or the keeper win the ball, they pass out of the box to their teammates who go at the opposite goal
- the teams switch roles if the counterattack is successful
- if the attackers miss the goal three times, the teams also change roles

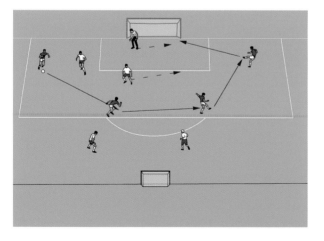

Positioning Near the Goal Line
Coaching points

- movement is composed but highly attentive
- move with short steps, always observing the ball
- cut the angle to the nearest post
- move forward to the nearest post as soon as the ball carrier dribbles into the box near the goal line
- see additional key points in "Narrowing the Goal Line"

Activity example
Organization:
- 2 big goals with a marked penalty box and one keeper each, 40 m opposite each other
- 2 groups of 4 players divided into 1 player on each wing and 2 players between the two penalty boxes

Objective:
- the keeper plays the ball to a wing player, who dribbles and crosses into the penalty box
- as the wing player dribbles, the midfield players run into the box to finish or to defend 2 vs. 2
- after each dead ball, the corresponding keeper plays the next ball to one of his wingers
- if the defenders win the ball, they pass out to one of their wing teammates for the next dribble and cross

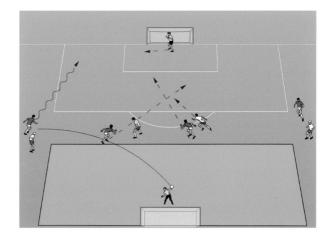

Positioning for Corner Kicks
Coaching points
- depending on the keeper, stand somewhere between the middle of the goal and about one step nearer to the far post
- one step off the goal line into the field
- face the ball at the corner
- observe and organize the players in front, be ready to come out for the ball
- secure the near post (often the far post as well) by putting a defender on the goal line

Activity example
Organization:
- 1 big goal with a keeper
- a marked counter line 35 m opposite the goal
- 2nd goalkeeper at the outside edge of the 6 yard box
- 3 attackers in front of the goal, 1 server at the corner, 4 players outside the box divided into 2 vs. 2

Objective:
- high corner kick to the far post (so the keeper being trained has a chance to get the ball)
- 3 attackers in the box try to finish with one touch only
- the 2nd keeper can catch or save the ball if it is played short (advantage for the keeper being trained)
- if one of the keepers catches the ball, they throw to one of the two attacking players outside the box who finish by dribbling over the counter line
- if the defending pair wins the ball, they pass to the server for next high cross into the box
- if successful in countering, the pair becomes the attacking players for the next repetition, otherwise switch roles after each goal and begin again with a serve from the corner

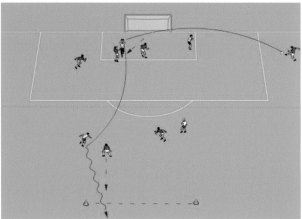

1 vs. the Goalkeeper (Breakaways)

Coaching points

- come out from the goal line slowly towards the ball carrier; always be ready to react sideways
- take short steps, observe only the movement of the ball
- make the body as big as possible by holding the hands out to the sides and standing firmly on both feet
- always be ready for a sudden shot
- delay the dribbling of the ball carrier (same as defenders)
- meet the attacker as far off the goal line as possible
- wait for the player's initiative as to which way he wants to pass
- if the ball is played to one side, step and dive immediately at the ball to catch it or push it away
- if the player hesitates, take advantage by diving at the ball immediately
- move hands toward the ball to save

Activity example

Organization:

- 1 big goal with 2 keepers
- 2 small goals, 2 m each, 25 m in front of the goal and 20 m apart from one another
- 6 players, each with a ball, divided in pairs right, left and center of the goal
- 1 recovering defender in each of the small goals

Objective:

- taking turns, each player dribbles 1 vs. the goalkeeper and attempts to score
- as soon as the player starts, one of the recovering defenders gives chase to assist the goalkeeper
- after each repetition, the player who shot runs back to his group and one from the next group starts
- the goalkeepers and the recovering defenders switch roles after each repetition
- if the goalkeeper or the recovering defender wins the ball, they counterattack on the 2 small goals and switch roles with the relevant attacker

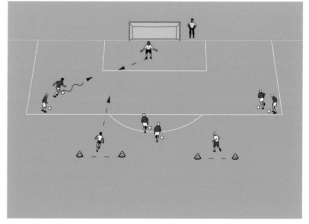

Jumping and Catching in the Air
Coaching points

- run forward out of the goal
- face the ball while running out to save a high cross
- take the most direct route to the spot where a field player could win the ball
- always take off with the leg closest to the ball
- use the other leg as a dynamic impulse for jumping and as a shield against approaching attackers
- catch the ball at its highest point possible
- if catching is too dangerous, punch it with one or both hands far out of the penalty area
- land on both feet

Activity example
Organization:

- 2 goals each with a keeper 30 m opposite each other
- 1 server with balls on each wing outside the box
- 4 attackers against 4 defenders in the penalty box

Objective:

- alternate high, long crosses from a server into the box
- play 4 vs. 4 to goal
- if the defenders or the keeper win the ball they counter on the opposite goal
- if the goalkeeper can not hold the ball then both teams play until a goal is scored
- if the attackers win the ball outside the box they must pass to a server for the next cross
- switch roles for both groups and the goalkeepers after about 10 crosses

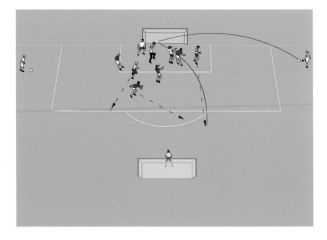

Leading – Organizing - Distributing
Coaching points

- short and clear commands of the keeper to draw the players' attention to special circumstances
- commands addressed to specific players, by name
- "keep cool" and radiate self-confidence
- only positive comments at all
- no arguments about missed assignments
- support the ball carrier diagonally behind him in order to safely change the point of attack
- control the ball and face the field before playing it
- play long, high balls into the attacking half when under pressure or when the defending team's fullbacks have moved up
- change the point of attack by passing the ball on the ground to a teammate

Activity example
Organization:

- marked field 30 x 50 m with a marked 30 m line
- 2 goals with 1 keeper each
- 8 players, divided into 3 vs. 2 in the 30 m zone and 1 vs. 2 in the 20 m zone

Objective:

- keep possession 3 vs. 2 in the 30 m zone
- the defending players can leave the 20 m zone to win the ball and finish
- the goalkeeper plays together with the 3 players in his zone and starts an attack with a long ball to the striker in the other zone who goes to the goal
- if the defending players win the ball, they counter on the opposite goal
- after each dead ball, a goal kick by the keeper into the 30 m zone restarts the play

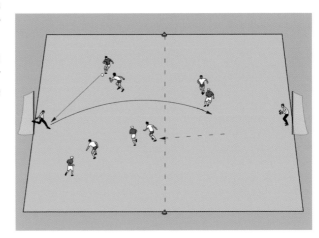

Psychological factors in the match influence the performance of the goalkeeper much more than that of a field player. This is due to the goalkeeper's position. There are no supporting players behind him. The consequences of a mistake made by the goalkeeper either lead to a goal or at least to a good scoring chance for the opponents. Keeping this in mind – and that the goalkeeper is reminded by the fans every time and again - his responsibility to both win and not to lose can lead to a fear of failure. The awareness of this high level of responsibility, not only for himself but also for the team, creates pressure. This pressure influences concentration and the coordination of basic movements, increasing the chance of making a mistake. This stress is much higher than what a field player has to deal with in a match. Training should then strengthen the self-confidence of the goalkeeper. Teaching positive visualizations is a great help. Activities and coaching should encourage the goalkeeper to take all risks required to save shots and defend the goal. The increase and maintenance of physical fitness should also be taken into account, as it's an important component of psychological strength and the ability to use all needed mental capacities successfully in the game.

7 AGILITY AND FLEXIBILITY ARE THE FOUNDATION OF PERFORMANCE

Research has shown that soccer players usually run more than five miles over a 90 minute duration. That's why fitness priority is placed first on **endurance**. Training aerobic as well as anaerobic endurance increases the ability to perform exercise at a higher overall intensity level during a match and minimizes the decline in technical performance that is induced by fatigue near the end of a game (T. REILLY & A. M. WILLIAMS, 2003).

One of the general principles of training requires those abilities which are needed (T. REILLY & A.M. WILLIAMS, 1999) to be trained and improved in the same way they are used in competition. Nearly all of soccer's required physical abilities are based on endurance, They can be practiced and improved by playing within different kinds of soccer games. The exceptions are maximum speed and flexibility. This is because to increase the level of these abilities always just a few seconds at maximal intensity are needed, followed by breaks long enough to fully recover the energy system. Those conditions don't really exist in a soccer game. Most runs are short sprints and are often influenced by the situation. The break inbetween the next action to be performed is not long enough to fully recover. Finally, movements impacting the flexibility (mobility) cannot be held long enough in exercises and mini-games to become effectively improved.

These fitness components depend on the strength and size of the muscles. The muscles, however, continue to grow through the final biological period of puberty. This typically occurs around the age of twelve. Therefore, there is no need to train power and elasticity with special drills prior to this period of biological development.

On the other hand, physical abilities which do not depend on muscle strength are appropriately trained at these ages simply through complex exercises and games typically used for improving technical and tactical abilities. This is based on the fact that the typical movements of a soccer player relate to getting possession of the ball, stopping, running, jumping, shooting and abruptly changing direction. For all these movements, however, the physical abilities of agility and flexibility are highly important.

The ability to jump into the air and divert a fast-moving ball with the head into a desired direction while observing the ongoing situation, and at the same time physically challenged by other players, requires the highest level of coordinative ability.

These kinds of physical abilities coordinate brain and muscles to lead the impulses for an action to the relevant muscles. The optimal performance of the muscles depends on its elasticity over the body's joints. However, elasticity decreases slowly from the beginning of life up to old age. Exercises a young child can perform without any problems are often too difficult for older people to perform. Thus; it is important concerning sports as well as health for children to continuously work on special exercises to improve stabilization, agility and flexibility.

All kinds of technical movements with the ball can be understood as kinds of coordinative exercises. However, these movements with the ball use only parts of the muscles and most of the lower body. So, a lot of cooperating muscles, in particular of the upper body, have to be trained. Accuracy and efficiency of the required movements in soccer depend on the level of agility, elasticity and flexibility of cooperating muscles in the entire body. The performance of technical movements in soccer increase and decrease with the level of coordinating abilities. This means that if there are deficits of fundamental agility, elasticity and flexibility, the player could not achieve his best technical level even if he is training technical drills long and hard. In short, coordinative abilities are the foundation of all technical movements not only in soccer but in all kinds of sports.

Thus, children's training has to be considered and therefore conducted with the goal of developing a wide and strong mental, psychological, physical and social base, not just best performances. From the beginning of playing soccer, in particular, within the years before the puberty changes the body and the mind, the training of children should consist of all kinds of running and catching games with and without a ball. Additionally, children of this age should do other complementary sports to improve coordinative development for a higher level of performance than adults. These kinds of sports could be all kinds of athletics, basketball, table tennis, hockey or just a lot of hours spent doing leisure sports.

8 PRINCIPLES OF TRAINING ARE THE GUIDELINES TO CONTINUOUS IMPROVEMENT

8.1 The Basic Principles of Training

There are some fundamental principles to be considered when preparing and running a training session. These principles serve as the basis for providing optimal learning conditions for the players as related to the individual stages of development, the season and the conditions associated with the particular day's practice. They should also be considered not only for planning one session, but additionally when designing weekly, monthly and seasonal plans.

The player should exercise only those elements which are required in the game soccer. And these elements should be exercised just in that kind as it is used in the game. This means, exercises should be constructed out of typical game situations relating to the topic to be improved.

Training Regularly
An increase in performance does not occur from one training session alone. A significant increase in the level of play requires a longer period of training in which the game's requirements are constantly repeated and progressively built upon each other. Playing too many games only reinforces bad habits.

Repeating Exercises
The most effective exercises are those which offer the opportunity for players to execute the topic to be improved more times than they would in an actual game. Exercises should also be repeated over a longer period of days and weeks.

Development-Based Training
The biological conditions necessary to permanently improve the different abilities needed in the game surface during different ages. Therefore, the contents and requirements of training need to be adapted according to the current stage of a players' development.

A short explanation of the objectives and corresponding activities of the training session in a motivational and encouraging manner promotes the successful implementation of the session.

Level-based Training

Exercises should challenge players to perform at their absolute best level. Easy, unassuming exercises impair concentration and attention. On the other hand, when players feel an exercise to be too difficult, they become resigned from the outset and stop trying all together.

Small Progressions from Simple to Complex

Exercises should relate to the players' level of efficiency. Once players consistently succeed in executing the given tasks, the exercises should then be modified and broadened step-by-step into more complex ones. Modifying an exercise with small steps supports the learning process. The player has to find solutions for only one or two new aspects within a familiar environment.

Periodical Variation Between Exercises with High and Low Intensity

Alternating exercises of high and low physical intensity helps players avoid getting tired too quickly. Lower intensity activities allow time for the body to recover. The body then compensates (to a certain degree) for the loss of energy which is ultimately needed. This leads to an improvement in fitness for the next game.

8.2 Organizational Aspects

Organizing always takes time. On one hand, this time can be viewed as a chance for players to recover from the last activity. On the other hand, this time usually takes away from available practice time. Therefore, organizing during the training session should take up as little time as possible. That means session organization, content and sequence have to be planned well in advance. Basic considerations for the planning of a training session include the number of players, their level of experience and development, available equipment and the size and quality of the training field. The most important aspect, however, should be planning the progressions and variations of the session in such a manner that time and ultimately confusion are kept to a minimum. The following are the critical key points to be taken into account for preparing a training session.

Small Groups
Small training groups present more opportunities for each player to contact the ball and get involved in ongoing practice situations. In particular, young and inexperienced players require relatively more space and time to improve their technical and tactical abilities in a low pressure environment.

Equipment
Balls, cones, bibs and other equipment should be seen as the player's "toys." Just like at home, players must take care of the equipment they need for training. The coach reminds them, gives orders or sometimes even shows where and how to take things to the field and put them back. Organizing in this way allows more control over what the players do with their time.

Activities
Players should not practice the same exercise more than 15-20 minutes. Doing the same thing over a long period of time leads to a decrease in motivation and concentration. Modifications to the session increase player motivation due to the new requirements that must be mastered.

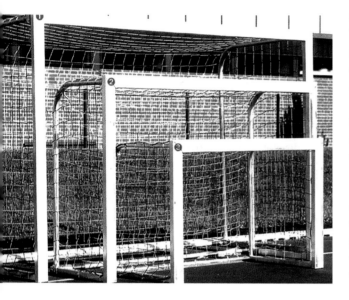

Goals

The crucial element in soccer is going to the goal. However, very often there are no full-sized goals available for practicing, sometimes not even small, mini-goals. In such cases, any practical way of marking a target can be used. Use poles, cones, bags and satchels as well as bibs to mark a particular line the ball should be played or dribbled over. How to score a goal – in other words how to be successful within a small game or an exercise – can be varied according to the specific training conditions.

Teams

Players from both teams should be marked by colored bibs when practicing in a more complex exercise or a small-sided game. This assists all players with the recognition of their environment and the conditions for making the necessary decisions. In a match, the more successful player is the one who is able to act faster, in a tactically and technically controlled manner.

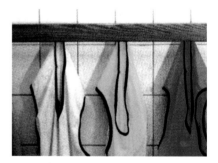

Ball

Anything round can be used as a ball. It should be able to roll and be solid enough to be kicked over distance, yet not too heavy or hard to play with. Even some old clothes knotted together in a somewhat round ball will suffice. Additionally, other kinds of balls like a tennis, plastic or rubber ball will get the job done.

8.3   Aspects of Modifying, Differentiating and Extending Exercises

In general, every exercise should be designed relative to the abilities of each player. If a player feels a task is too easy he might lose the motivation to practice seriously. This results in a reduction in concentration, which leads to a decrease in the speed of improvement. If he feels a task is too difficult for him, he will lose the motivation to practice at all. The most effective motivation to perform a given task is developed when a player believes he can do something, yet is not entirely certain he can perform successfully. Hence, exercises have to be differentiated according to the players' level. Since there may be a significant variation in players' abilities feel free to impose a more difficult restriction on more able players or a reduced requirement for a player of less skill (see "variations" in chapter 5). By all means make individual adjustments that help players capitalize on strengths or correct deficiencies. Basically, any exercise can be modified in several ways. Each modification relates to both attacking and defending players. If you make a task easy for one of them, you automatically make it harder for the other. The following table presents a short overview of the factors and aspects of activity modification.

Goal:	• a bigger goal is easier to attack than a smaller one
	• more goals are easier to attack than just one goal
Players:	• attacking with numerical majority is easier than with equal numbers
	• attacking with equal numbers is easier than with numerical minority
	• training without an opponent is easier than with one
Space:	• attacking in larger spaces is easier than in smaller ones
Time:	• training without a time limit is easier than under the pressure of time
Tasks:	• attacking without special rules is easier than with them
	• training only one aspect is easier than training multiple aspects
	(reversing these principles would focus on modifications for defenders)

If, for example, the player in possession is constantly succeeding and of the ball is unable to successfully complete a task, although having tried his best several times, then the task has to be modified into an easier one. This can be done by restricting the defending situation for the opponent (i.e. to defend a line rather than a smaller goal or space, to reduce the number of opponents).

If, however, the player or team in possession has consistently succeeded and the defensive team is unable to regain possession, then the exercise has to be modified into a more difficult one. More difficult in this case means more complex conditions which approach the real conditions of the game. This can be achieved by increasing pressure through a time restriction, limiting the space available to play in as well as playing against a numerical majority rather than equal or less defensive numbers. The same modification procedure can be used when the topic focuses on improving defending abilities.

9 WELL-STRUCTURED TRAINING SUPPORTS SUCCESSFUL PERFORMANCE

9.1 General Aspects

A training session should basically be divided into three parts. The first part of 15 to 20 minutes is used to warm up. Here, the body will be prepared for the load it is to undergo in the subsequent sections of the practice. Younger children do not need specific exercises for physical preparation due to their generally higher blood pressure. A specific **warm-up** plan becomes necessary as children develop through puberty (around 12 years of age).

The final component of a training unit should be focused on **cooling down**. In general, this time is used to help the body "regenerate" itself following the intense strain it has been put under. Jogging and stretching typically comprise a portion of this section. Prior to cooling down, it is important that the players have a simple match without any rules, restrictions or modifications. The purpose here is for them to have some fun at the end of training before the cool-down. Children under 12 years of age do not need a specific cool-down component for the same reasons mentioned above regarding warming up.

The main body of the training session, of course, would then be comprised of the time period between the warm-up and cool-down. In order to implement this part of training in a most efficient manner, a few basic principles should be considered:

Early and consistent training of basic coordination skills as the foundation for any kind of technical movement is an important part of player progress and success.

Activities which require the **highest anaerobic load** should be utilized directly after having finished the warm-up, prior to a player becoming fatigued. In this category are topics such as sprinting, shooting, jumping and concentration through high-repetition skill work.

Exercises requiring an **aerobic load** can implemented at the end of the main body of training just before the cool down. These exercises could be smaller games with a larger number of players or desired tactical movements to be trained and repeated.

There should be a permanent **alternation of exercises** between those which are anaerobic and aerobic. This is due to the need for the body to reproduce energy after a high-intensity load in order to recover before performing the next high-intensity task.

A training session for children up to seven years of age should not last more than about 60 minutes. Children cannot concentrate over a longer period of time. A training unit for older players should not last more than 90 to 100 minutes. However, it is important to practice more than once a week in order to give players as many opportunities as possible for learning and repeating.

9.2 Structure of a Basic Training Session

The following table presents the general structure of a training unit according to the basic principles and aspects of training. In order to work efficiently and successfully, no more than two topics should be trained in one session. Players need time to discover and gain experience in a specific topic. More than two topics in the same session defeats this purpose.

A:	Warm-up		(about 20 min)
B:	**Main Body of Training**		**(about 70 min)**
	1st learning aspect:	small game (own experiences)	(5 min)
		activity (of particular aspect)	(15 min)
		small game (repetition)	(6 min)
	Motivational task	(agility exercise, i.e. tag games)	(5 min)
	2nd learning aspect:	(repetition of last sessions)	
		activity	(15 min)
		small game	(6 min)
	Final match:	(all together)	(15 min)
C:	Cool-down		(about 10 min)

9.3 Preparation of a Basic Training Session

Training is a systematical process for improving mental and physical abilities. Systematical training is characterized by two key points:
- **Continuity** - training one objective for more than just one or two sessions
- **Progress** - to incrementally increase the requirements for specific activities

In other words, it does not make any sense to change objectives and topics from one training session to another. Training should be constructed in periods of four to six weeks in which the players can improve a specific objective step-by-step. Combining two objectives to be improved could be arranged by changing the objective every two to three weeks. Together with a mixture of exercises, such a variation of topics and objectives guarantees long-term training motivation.
Typically one mid-term goal for a team will be combined in a session together with an urgent problem which has been analyzed in a previous match. In this way just one or two week's sessions focus on the solution of an urgent problem. Other training areas which lack progress may then need to be addressed by special exercises. Systematical training in this sense means one longer-termed objective will be combined with other short-term topics which focus on the next game.

The foundation of all successful systematic training sessions is the careful preparation of each practice.
However, preparing a session does not mean to plan in detail all aspects of time, groupings and exercises in advance. Several unpredictable circumstances sometimes require the coach to improvise on the spot. Preparing a training session should therefore be understood as a rudimentary concept. As such, some general aspects need to be considered:

- the objective and its particular link to the last session's topic
- the level of the players in relation to the objective
- particular observations from the last game which need to be improved
- the quality and size of the available training field
- the number of players expected for this training session
- available equipment

Some important considerations help one avoid spending additional organizational time during the training session:
- Which type of exercises should be used?
- How should the exercises be sequenced (regarding the basic principles of training)?

- How can things be organized to guarantee quick, simple changes of the exercises (without having to rebuild each activity)?
- How can the session be modified in case a player is missing?

The duration of the exercises should be considered in a "rough" manner. In reality it depends on the motivation, the improvement and the physical stage of the players. There is no need to always stick exactly to that which has been prepared. Sometimes the ongoing session suggests staying with one exercise for more time and perhaps eliminating another due to a lack of time. That eliminated activity could then be easily implemented into the next training session.

The following sample shall demonstrate ideas and considerations for preparing a training session. This example is for players between 12 and 14 years of age.

9.4   Sample Sessions

Organizational plan

The field for this session will be set up as follows:
- 2 zone lines to be marked by small cones or old bibs (red)
- 1 corner line marked by small cones (red)
- 1 portable goal in the middle of the defending zone line, 25 m opposite the 2nd goal

This can be easily done by the players within two minutes before warming up. There is no need for further organization beyond this, which of course saves time for training.

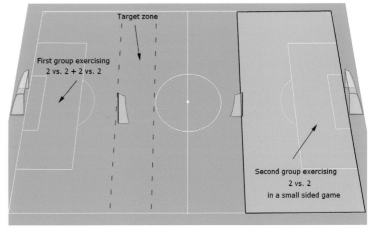

Warm-up (about 20 minutes)

Pairs of players with one ball each. Pass and move. Rehearse slow repetitions of combination runs (i.e. wall pass, overlap, crossover).

Objective taken from analysis of previous games: *"Finishing through the center of the field"*
Special topic: *strikers support for a wall pass*
Based on players' level: *play 2 vs. 2 through the center*

Game situation: 2 vs. 2 wall pass
The selected area for improvement:
Coaching points:

- spacing diagonally towards the dribbling player
- keeping an eye on the ball carrier
- check off the defending player to support
- support for 2 vs. 1 play
- run towards the ball carrier when he is close to the opponent and able to play
- run straight towards the ball
- shield the ball against the opponent
- one-touch pass or dribble zone

Construction of an appropriate exercise taken from a game situation:

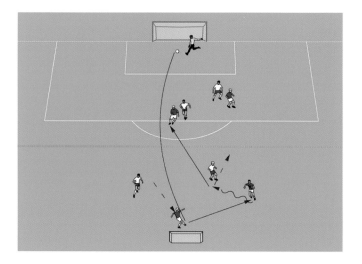

- 1 big goal with a goalkeeper
- 1 counter goal, 4 m wide, 35 m opposite the big goal
- 8 players, distributed into 2 pairs 1 vs. 1 in the midfield and 2 pairs in front of the box
- one of the attacking midfielders asks for the ball after the other midfielder received the ball from the goalkeeper's kick, take turns
- after gaining ball control, the midfielder tries to score a goal while supported by one striker at the penalty area
- if the midfielder gets under pressure, he passes back to his teammate for a change of roles
- obligation: each midfielder is supported by only one striker
- after each kind of finish, the keeper plays the ball to the opposite goal to start the next attack
- if the defender wins the ball, counter on the opposite goal supported by the defenders of the alternative pairs

Possible modifications:
- Midfielders can play together with one pass only, no return pass
- Strikers can play together with one pass only, no return pass
- Defenders can support each other

Organization in training: (about 30 minutes including time to change)
- Small-sided games "2 vs. 2 on two goals" (teams divided into 4 pairs each, change after each goal scored, about 6 minutes)
- Practicing: Two groups of 8 players, the same exercise as described on two different goals (about 15 minutes)

Motivational task for the whole group (about 5 minutes)
Shooting
- two groups of players and one goalkeeper, each player with one ball
- alternate shots from different spots outside of the box with two touches against the goalkeeper of the other group
- keep track of which group scores the most

Objective to be improved over a longer period of time:
"Keeping possession of the ball"
Special topic:
the build-up of an attack with a numerical majority
Based on players' level:
play 5 vs. 3

Game situation:
Coaching points:

- safe passes for ball possession first
- use the width and depth of the field
- play longer passes
- slow down the pace of play
- avoid one vs. one situations
- run to support, always facing the ball
- easy passes to feet

Player not needed for exercising the topic transition from defense to attack are marked

The objective of keeping possession of the ball has been practiced and the players have already experienced and improved the basic topics.
Therefore, both exercises are combined into a more complex one of building up out of the back and finishing supported by one striker.

Construction of an appropriate exercise taken from a game situation:
- 1 big goal with a goalkeeper
- a target zone 5 m deep, 30 m ahead of the goal
- 5 defenders and 3 attackers
- three attackers go for the goal against five defenders after having taken the finished ball out of the target zone
- if ball is won, defenders attack into the target zone
- the target is achieved when the ball is passed to a teammate within the zone (to leave it for the next attack)
- the attackers are not allowed to move into the zone

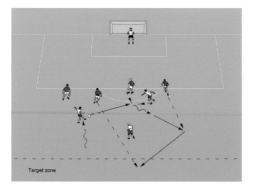

Target zone

Recovering break (about 5 minutes): Refresh, stretch

Combined complex exercise 5 – 3 + 2 – 2 on two goals

Organization of the exercise: (about 25 minutes)

- a marked target zone, 5 m deep, touching the center circle in one half of the field with one big goal on the goal line
- another big goal in the opposite half, on a marked line, 25 m behind the midline
- 5 vs. 3 in the target zone, and 2 vs. 2 + 2 vs. 2 in the opposite halfObjectives:

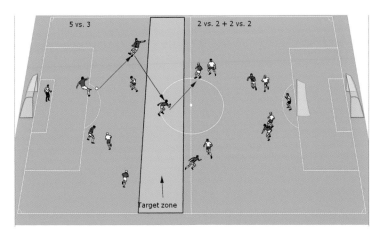

- each new exercise will be started by a long goal kick by the goalkeeper over the target zone into the other half of the field to his 2 strikers in order to attack the opposite goal
- if the 5 defending players win the ball, they attack towards the target zone
- an opponent is not allowed to move into the target zone
- as soon as one of the 5 defending players controls the ball in the target zone, he can play the ball to one of his midfielders in the opposite part of the field to start their attack 2 vs. 2 + 2 vs. 2 on the opposite goal
- if the defenders win the ball, they counterattack towards the opposite goal

Final concept of the training session:

Warm-up			about 15 min

Training	1st topic:	"support of the striker"	**about 25 min**
		1 vs. 1 + 1 vs. 1 on 1 goal	
		Small-sided game	
		Exercise	
	Motivational task: shooting		**about 5 min**
	2nd topic	"transition"	**about 15 min**
		5 vs. 3 in defense	
	Recovering break: refreshments and stretching		
	Combined exercise:		**about 15 min**
		5 vs 3 + 2 vs 2 + 2 vs 2 on two goals	

Final match			about 15 min

Cool-down			about 10 min

10 APPENDIX

Specific Coaching Points Support Coaching Based on Facts

The following topics to be improved from the practice chapter (6.2) are listed in alphabetical order. The pictures act to clarify the general idea of the topic's situational meaning. Each topic is marked with the number of the exercise in which it can be successfully improved as part of a typical, yet specific game situation. Therefore, the same topics are described using different key points of execution. This is due to the different situations which are used as models of the described exercise. The exercises are numbered in the same manner to simplify the link to the topic's detailed key points of execution.

Receiving balls on the ground (1)
- move towards the ball
- slow down just before touching the ball
- keep body between ball and defender
- planted leg's knee is slightly bent
- control the ball one step from the body with the first touch
- "give" with the receiving foot when first contacting the ball
- with the first touch step to the ball
- following the first touch, step in the direction of the ball

Receiving balls in the air (1)
plant leg (on the ground):

- take and move the ball with the first touch
- touch the ball right after it hits the ground
  (don't let it bounce back up)
- cover the ball with the inside or outside of the foot, which is slanted over the ball just before it hits the ground (half-volley)

receiving with the chest:
- both feet on the ground, knees slightly bent
- lean towards the ball and give once the ball touches the body
- elbows back, body stable *(in the air)*

Receiving: (3)
- check-off run when asking for the ball to get away from the defender
- body feint before receiving the ball to gain further space and time
- take and move the ball with the first touch
- if space permits, turn, face the defender and take him on

Receiving (4)
- body feint, move towards the ball as it is about to be played
- first touch takes the ball back or to the side of the defender into a move
- if space permits, turn, face the defender and take him on
- shield the ball, if needed, using the shoulder against the defender
- some situations call for putting the ball behind the defender on first touch

Receiving (18)
- move the ball away from the opponent
- always keep an eye on the field and teammates
- observe the movements of the striker in front when getting the ball
- avoiding one vs. one situations with opponents

Combining (6)
Crossover or dribble
- from a position in front of or equal to the level of the ball, switch quickly by crossing the ball carrier's path to the goal

Crossover or dribble

- time the decision to pass or dribble as soon as the supporting player crosses behind the defender
- decide to pass the ball into the run of the supporting player if defender covers the dribble; decide to dribble if the defender covers the passing lane to the supporting player
- once decision is made, either attack the defender quickly or immediately offer new support to player with ball

Overlap or dribble

- from a starting position behind the ball carrier, quickly run behind the ball carrier away from the ball's direct path towards the goal (defender has to cover the most dangerous space)

Overlap or dribble

- time the decision to pass or to dribble as soon as the supporting player passes the level of the ball
- decide to pass the ball into the supporting player's run straight toward the goal if the defender covers the direct path to the goal or to dribble straight toward the goal if defender covers the passing lane to the supporter
- ball carrier takes the ball inside towards the goal to shorten the length of the supporting player's run

Wall pass or dribble

- from a position in front of the ball carrier nearer to the goal, make a quick and short run directly towards the ball to support like a "wall" to beat the ball carrier's opponent
- decide to run and support as soon as the ball carrier dribbles at the defender
- decide to pass if defender covers the direct path straight to the goal; decision to beat the opponent by dribbling if he covers the passing lane to the supporting player
- easy, on-ground pass to the feet of the supporter followed by immediate sprint behind opponent to get the ball back

Takeover or dribble

- dribble straight at the supporting player while shielding the ball on one side against the defender

- decide to take over the ball if the opponent keeps on moving forward next to the ball carrier or to keep and dribble if the opponent stops his run expecting the takeover
- shield the ball with the shoulder against the opponent
- dribble the ball with the foot furthest to the opponent in order for the supporting player to take the ball easily

Communication (15)

- always coach the teammates beside and in front of you
- call loudly, using names and giving short, clear commands
- guide, don't commentate
- be very specific

Security in attack (14)
- every attack must have support from behind the level of the ball
- support from behind on one side from of greater distance
- if being challenged, keep ball possession by passing it back to a teammate
- communicate with the ball carrier from behind

Creating/using space (12)
- keep distance, diagonally from each other to create 1 vs. 1 situations
- support the ball carrier by creating depth in front of the ball
- create options by running off with the ball in close situations
- run diagonally into the center, always observing the ball

Creating space (14)
- support in front of and beside the ball
- keep distance to the ball to create space and make defenders run longer when ball is passed
- after controlling the ball, first look to pass forward
- use space to dribble, even diagonally if the ball cannot be played forward

Crossing (3)
- short bent run to the ball before crossing to get beside it and have a better look into the penalty area
- observe the moves of the players in the center in order to decide how and where to cross the ball
- play the ball close to the standing leg
- play the bottom half of the ball with the inside of the foot for crosses in the air, with the full instep for crosses on the ground (driven ball)

Crossing (13)
- cross the ball on the ground behind the opponents if there is space between them and the goal (i.e. counterattack situation)
- short, on-ground crosses behind a recovering defense to trailing teammates
- if the defense is positioned compact in and around the penalty area, crosses in the air played early to the far post for heading
- powerful crosses (on the ground and in the air) straight through the box or bent away from the goal (more difficult to defend)

Crossing (17)
- play crosses on the ground from the endline behind the defenders' backs
- observe the moves of the center attacker and supporting midfielder before crossing
- play hard crosses into the teammates' run
- use the "weak foot" to cross if needed in order to prevent the defense from organizing

Defending (1)
- challenge the ball at once if the ball carrier tries to beat the defender on the covered side (keep the covered side closed)
- turn and challenge the ball as soon as the opponent has played it into the space behind the defender
- challenge the ball while running in the same direction as the opponent
- try to cross the path of the opponent to the ball and take the ball from the side
- use the body while running to the ball to take the opponent's run away from the desired direction
- play the ball out of the opponent's control when getting to the ball at the same time as the opponent

Defending (13)

- offer the weak side to the touchline while delaying (touch line as second defender!)
- cover the shortest distance to the goal as long as the second defender still is approaching
- double-team the ball carrier as soon as his most dangerous path to the goal (shortest route) is covered by the first defender
- attack the ball from the side when in a majority situation
- delay without pressure on the ball to win time for the teammates to recover and support

Defending against numerical majority (5)

- delay the ball carrier and supporting attacker from moving toward the goal to win time for other defenders
- trap the ball carrier into a one vs. one situation (avoiding the pass) when delaying
- cover the lane to the goal against a penetrating pass or dribble
- challenge the ball carrier as soon as he approaches the shooting area

Defending against numerical majority (6)

- always cover the ball carrier's shortest route to the goal
- cover the nearest attacker to the goal, never leave an attacker in the space behind (exception: offside trap)
- force the attacker to play the ball square or slow down his dribble
- offer the space away from the goal for the attacker to go in (make it very obvious)

Delaying (1)

- cover the route to the goal while delaying
- offer a route away from the goal to induce the ball carrier to use it.
- move backwards with a staggered stance to slow down the speed of the ball carrier
- delay just one step ahead of the opponent
- watch the ball only, with no reaction to any body feints
- wait for the decision of the ball carrier as to which side he wants to to pass
- always be ready to take advantage of an opponent's mistake

Delaying (2)
- move quickly towards the ball carrier before he gains control to pick him up as far away from the goal as possible (creates space to delay)
- slow down as the ball carrier approaches, leave some distance from the ball carrier and delay as he dribbles toward the opponent
- cover the attacker's passing lane to his teammate so he can't pass to another attacker behind the delaying defender
- transition quickly by dribbling or passing the ball to the teammate after having won the ball

Delaying (15)
- cover the space close to the attacker to put him under pressure and force mistakes
- delay in the space between the attacker and the goal to force the ball back and square
- delay the ball carrier from the side to force the attack to a desired wing and close the space for double-teaming
- cover the lane to the central attacker to avoid penetrating passes behind the defense

Delaying (16)
- move backwards, holding the offside line to slow down the pace of the counterattack
- force the ball carrier to dribble and keep ball possession to win time for recovering teammates
- cover the space to the goal close to the supporting attackers to create opportunities to win the ball back
- take risks and challenge the ball when the ball carrier has reached shooting distance

Delaying (18)
- challenge the ball carrier, covering the deep spaces behind the defense in front of own goal
- recover back diagonally into deep areas away from the ball to cover spaces when a square pass is played
- tackle the ball only when it's not under control by the attacker
- coach the supporting player in front

Delaying (19)

- cover the space between the ball and the striker in front of the goal to prevent passes to him
- shift according to the movement of the ball
- delay, looking for any option to intercept a pass or for the opponent's mistake
- mark the striker in the back of him to avoid passes in the space behind the defender

Double-teaming/challenging the ball (11)

- double-team at the touchline or by pushing the ball carrier to the touch line
- the first defender delays by covering the route towards the goal keeping the attacker in possession of the ball (to allow time for the next defender)
- quick attack from the side or from behind the attacker to the ball by the doubling opponent
- delaying defender follows and challenges the ball from the same direction as soon as the ball carrier chooses one side to pass him while the other defender follows close behind covering the attacker's option to turn back

Double-teaming (13)

- cover each other keeping no more than two steps distance when doubling the ball carrier
- double-team the ball carrier to the side where he could pass the ball to another teammate
- when you have cover, tackle the ball in that moment when the ball carrier has to move the ball first before making a safe pass
- if the ball carrier dribbles into the space beside the defender, the second defender then follows him to avoid a sudden turn while the first defender attacks the ball from the same running direction

Dribbling (1)

- dribble with the inside of the foot diagonally across the body; with the outside of the foot diagonally away from the body (feinting)
- dribble with the outside of the foot straight ahead (speed)
- dribble to the side of the opponent to force him to move
- keep your speed but also keep the ball under control when dribbling against an opponent (don't lose time)
- tempt the opponent with a feint by stepping to the side first

Dribbling (2)

- dribble into the space beside the opponent to force him to move
- dribble with speed to make the most of any delay by the opponent to pass him
- observe the movements of supporting teammates to recognize spaces to use or better options to pass the ball
- keep eye contact with each other

Dribbling (3)

- dribble from the touchline toward the center to create space on the touchline and to force the opponent to move
- dribble straight toward the opponent to create two suitable options to get past him
- keep head up to observe actions in and around the box
- quick decision to beat the opponent and get in the space behind him

Dribbling: (4)

- dribble to the side with the body between the ball and defender if less space is available or after a body feint with subsequent speed if space is available
- make body contact with the defender to control ball, turn and dribble using the defenders body
- dribble into space in order to force the defender to move (gain time and easier control of ball)
- dribble diagonally toward the goal to create space for penetrating passes

Dribbling (15)

- dribble away from the opponent into space to create options for penetrating passes
- always look for opportunities to play to teammates in front who can beat midfield opponents
- avoid one vs. one situations in midfield
- dribble with moderate speed in order to still observe movements of teammates

Dribbling (17)

- after controlling the ball, dribble straight toward the opponent, away from the touchline to create space for one vs. one's and support by teammates
- quick dribble, quick decisions whether to go one vs. one or pass
- observe movements of teammates in the center and up front
- use the space behind the defender (if no covering defender) to beat him one vs. one

Dribbling (19)

- dribble quickly into the space between the opponents to open covered space for penetrating passes
- dribble with moderate speed in order to still observe movements of teammates
- dribble away from opponents to avoid one vs. one situations
- always face teammates in front

Dribbling against numerical majority (11)

- shield the ball with the body (shoulder) against the challenging defender while moving slowly with the first touch
- move away from the opponent into open space when deciding to delay and wait for supporting players
- dribble to the side not covered by the first defender to tempt the second defender to change position to create the opportunity to feint and break through
- split both defenders with a dribble if they defend at the same level beside each other (flat)

Feinting move (1) step over:

- a wide step over the ball diagonally to one side, feinting to dribble past on the opposite side
- observe the reaction of the defender while feinting
- play the ball behind the defender on the other side with the outside of the opposite foot, and explode behind the defender if he moves to the feinted side ("buys" the move)
- play the ball behind the defender on the feinted side with the inside of the opposite foot if the opponent closes the space on the feinted side (doesn't "buy" the move)
- keep space between the ball and the opponent when starting the feint (don't get too close)

Finishing (3) OPTIONS

(1) • move towards the ball carrier to support him (wall pass)
(2) • delay run by waiting at top of penalty area, then go straight to the nearest post as soon as the ball carrier is ready to cross
(3) • run at the crossed ball to cut the defender's path and get there first
(4) • make a quick pass to the advancing midfielder if there is not a successful scoring opportunity

Finishing (12)

1. • take any risk to shoot as soon as within shooting distance
2. • run at a crossed ball to beat the defender and shoot quickly
3. • when marked, perform a body feint (fake) and sprint towards the ball taking a route that cuts the defenders path to the ball
4. • when marked tightly, shield the ball by using the body (shoulder) against the opponent's body in order to control the ball, feint and turn

Finishing (16)

1. • hard, on-ground passes as assists
2. • attempt to finish by shooting at any realistic opportunity
   • follow the shot in case of any rebounds from the goalkeeper
3. • use the numerical majority by playing to the unmarked teammate

Marking (2)

- move close to the attacker to be able to intercept the ball if passed
- keep the advantage by blocking the shortest way to the goal while moving
- always observe both the ball and the opponent
- transition quickly and counter as soon as the ball is won

Marking (3)

- always observe both the ball and the opponent
- always defend the shortest route to the goal as the striker moves
- give space to the striker as he moves away from the ball
- cover the striker very tightly the closer he comes to the ball

Marking (4)
- on the ball side close to the opponent, avoiding body contact
- intercept the ball if opponent does not go to it
- follow the opponent to the ball, close enough so that he cannot turn to face the defender when receiving it
- wait for the opponent's decision if and to which side to dribble before challenging the ball

Marking (11)
- if the attacker is still waiting for the ball, mark him with a defender beside him ready to disrupt the pass and the other defender behind the attacker to cover the challenge of the pass by his teammate
- mark beside the attacker on the "ball-side", that is, where the ball can be played straight to the goal
- observe both the ball and the attacker, be ready for both a pass and/or movement by the attacker
- avoid body contact with the attacker while marking him and be ready for interrupting the pass, unhindered

Marking (12)
- the player delaying the ball carrier is covered by the second defender who stands diagonally to the side of the second attacker
- delay by forcing the ball carrier away from the goal
- cut the option to the second attacker by challenging the ball from that side (interrupting the square pass option)
- mark all other attackers in front of the ball tightly

Marking/taking over (14)
- mark the opponent tightly, ready intercept a pass to him
- mark on the more dangerous side to the goal
- follow the moving opponent on his side up to the next free defender and back into the left zone (space)
- take over a moving opponent one step closer to the own goal (behind the teammate)

Marking/covering (17)

- mark any attacker in front of the ball tightly
- cover the most dangerous space for the ball to get to the goal
- always mark the central attacker on the most dangerous side
- do not allow the supporting central attacker into the space behind the defense

Offside trap (14)

- move forward quickly, leaving the opponent in offside position when the ball is played back over a longer distance and cannot be played immediately forward
- move forward to put an opponent in offside position if the ball carrier turns with his back to the goal
- challenge the ball immediately when using an offside trap
- follow the opponent running into an offside position one step behind and be ready to defend if offside isn't whistled

Passing (15)

- pass to the feet of a moving teammate for quick ball control
- play on-the-ground passes which are easy to control and don't waste time
- play hard balls to win time for a safe and controlled build- up of the attack
- use short and precise passes when combining

Passing (18)

- pass the ball on the ground when possible
- give proper speed (weight) to the ball when passing it
- pass the ball to the feet of teammates so they can quickly control it
- play long balls to give time for teammates to safely bring the ball under control

Shifting (15)
- always shift to the side on which the ball is
- shift diagonally backwards to keep the space to the goal covered
- while midfielders shift to the ball side, one player must get into the line between the ball and the goal and move to the ball to delay
- while shifting, always look for opportunities to disrupt the play and win the ball

✳ Shooting: (1)
- <u>shoot as soon as an opportunity presents itself</u>
- shoot with the <u>instep from greater distances</u>
- <u>use the foot which is able to shoot earlier / quicker</u> in a given situation
- <u>look for opening in the goal</u>
- <u>follow the shot in case of a rebound</u>
- use the <u>inside of the foot for short-distance shots</u>
- <u>beat the goalkeeper</u>, <u>if he comes out</u>, by <u>dribbling and feinting</u> *+ CHIP SHOT !*

Supporting (2)
- run to support the ball carrier diagonally from the goal side so that the defender can be cut-off upon receiving the ball
- use a body feint or check off when running to support the ball carrier
- sprint to support when the ball carrier can observe the move and is able to play the ball immediately
- cross the path of the ball carrier to take the defender away and create space for him to dribble and finish

Supporting : (4)
- diagonally follow the pass to the strikers, be ready to combine with him and cover the space behind them
- move to the side to create space so the receiver can control and dribble
- support in the space where the ball carrier can look and play
- support quickly in order to get recognized by the ball carrier

Supporting (5)
- face the ball carrier – establish eye contact
- draw the defender into a one vs. one situation (near the ball) before deciding to pass or take him on
- "uncover" the defender to receive an on-ground pass without risk
- control the played ball with the first touch leading to a dribble towards the goal

Supporting (6)
- quickly switch positions with the ball carrier (defender's decision of who to follow)
- run in the area where the ball is to combine
- quick decision and quick run (less time for the defender to challenge the ball)
- always watch both the ball and ball carrier while running to support

Supporting (11)
- seek eye contact with the ball carrier and support from an uncovered space in which the ball can be played on the ground
- support quickly to shorten the time for the defender to challenge the ball
- give a loud but short verbal call to the ball carrier to make him aware of your supporting run
- if too close, run off the ball into a space toward the opponents' goal to force a defender to follow

Supporting (12)
- runs: sprint before the ball is played
- short "dummy run" to check off the defender
- run to support when the ball carrier can observe the run and play the ball
- continue to run to support after having played the ball

Supporting (13)
- keep away from the ball carrier for a safe back-pass option
- move sideways in the midfield into a space to offer an option for a safe square pass
- quick run to offer a combination to beat the opponent
- run away from the ball carrier to lure a defender and create attacking space

Supporting (14)
- correspond to both sides when combining
- no movement to the hidden side before taking action
- attack with convincing movements to the expected side
- observe the opponents' behavior to guide the decision-making process

Supporting (15)
- use the entire space when supporting the ball carrier
- run into spaces in which the ball can be played on the ground
- create a numerical majority around the ball by quickly following the pass
- quickly check off the defender to support to the ball carrier

Supporting (16)
- create and use a numerical majority on the wings
- pass into spaces between defenders to beat a defense playing offside
- quick combinations
- give support for a safe pass to avoid a one vs. one situation

Supporting (17)
- checking runs to create space and time for safe ball control
- quick runs to clarify desired options for combining with the ball carrier
- change positions (cross) with the ball carrier to reduce (lessen) the defender's covered space to the goal
- support the ball carrier for wall passes from the center to assist with a build-up of the attack in the wing

Supporting (18)
- use the space toward the touchlines to avoid the defender challenging the ball
- always face the ball while running to support
- support wide and deep to the ball carrier
- clear the zone covered by the strikers to enable an on-ground pass

Supporting (19)
- preserve the attack by supporting behind the ball carrier
- create and use space in depth for beating opponents with penetrating passes
- create and use space in width for changing the point of attack
- follow the ball immediately after having passed it to a teammate in front to support again

Tackling (1)

- play the ball before any contact with the opponent
- attack the ball with one leg
- attack the ball from the side or same direction as the ball carrier is dribbling
- play the ball out of the control and run of the ball carrier
- slide into the run of the ball to stop and possibly keep it
- play the ball with the instep or inside of the foot
- attack the ball when the opponent cannot reach it with his next step
- attack the ball when close to it

Transition : (4)

- dribble quickly with the ball forward and away from the opponent as soon as having won the ball or immediately pass it to an open teammate who can counter
- safe and easy passes when countering
- avoid one vs. one situations, use space
- support to open the field when countering

Transition (12)

- having lost possession, the player nearest the ball must immediately recover to the most direct route for the ball carrier and/or his first passing option, including a back pass
- the second player drops and covers the midfield space, forcing the ball carrier to pass square
- having lost possession, immediately chase as long as possession isn't yet secured by the opponents
- move in order to interrupt the opponents' changing the point of attack

Transition (13)

- play the ball out of the area where it was won back to an unmarked teammate to keep possession before starting an attack
- run away from the player who won the ball to open space and offer safe passing options
- shield the ball with the body and dribble into space to keep it and look for a safe option to maintain possession
- if there is space behind the defenders, dribble quickly and use it for starting a counterattack

11 REFERENCES

Bandura, A. (1999). Social cognitive theory of personality; in: *Handbook of personality. Theory and Research;* Gilford Press, New York.

Bandura, A. (1999). *Self-efficacy: Towards a unifying theory of behavioural change;* Psychology Press, Taylor & Francis.

Bisanz, G. (2002) Success in Soccer, Vol. 1 , *Basic training*, Philippka, Münster/W.

Bisanz, G. (2002) Success in Soccer, Vol. 2, *Advanced Training*, Philippka, Münster/W.

Brueggemann, D. (2003). Fußball Handbuch, Band 3: *Coaching*, Hofmann, Schorndorf

Brueggemann, D. (1999). Fußball Handbuch, Band 2: *Kinder- und Jugendtraining,* Hofmann, Schorndorf.

Brueggemann, D. / Albrecht, D. (2003). Fußball Handbuch, Band 1; 5. neu überarbeitete Auflage: *Modernes Fußballtraining*, Hofmann, Schorndorf.

Brueggemann, D./ Fathi, M. (2003). Soccer-Guide, Volume 1: *Parents' Guide;* Authorhouse, Bloomington, USA

Duda, J.L., (1993), Goals: A social cognitive approach to the study of achievement motivation in sport. In: *Handbook of Research in Sport Psychology*, Macmillan, New York.

Duda, J.L. (1996). Maximizing motivation in sport and physical education among children and adolescents: the case for greater task involvement, in: *Quest*.

Goleman, D. (1995): *Emotional Intelligence*, Bantam Books, New York.

Goleman, D.; Kaufman, P; Ray, M. (1993) *The Creative Spirit*, Penguin Books.

Hurrelmann, K. (1999). *Lebensphase Jugend. Eine Einführung in die sozialwissenschaftliche Jugendforschung*. Juventa, Weinheim.

Oerter, R. / Montada, L. (Hrsg.), (2002). *Entwicklungspsychologie*, Beltz, Weinheim.

Reilly, T. / Williams, A.M. (2003). *Science and Soccer, 2nd ed*. Routledge, London.

Williams, A.M. (2000). Perceptual skill in soccer: implications for talent identification and development. *Journal of Sports Sciences. 18*.

Williams, J.M. (1998). *Applied Sport Psychology: Personal Growth to Peak Performance,* 3rd ed., Mayfield, Mountain View, CA.